"In this original book of essays, Harold Kasimow provides an intimate portrait of Abraham Joshua Heschel's prophetic commitment to interreligious dialogue, nonviolence, social justice, and the power of faith to transform the heart. A former student of Heschel, Kasimow covers unexplored themes in Heschel scholarship: including Heschel's unique view of revelation, religious pluralism, and the Holocaust; his friendship with Martin Luther King, Jr., possible influence on Pope Francis, and affinity with the spirituality of Swami Vivekananda. One of the most compelling chapters is 'Spiritual Masters in the Jewish Tradition,' in which Kasimow situates Heschel within the tradition of Jewish saints, emphasizing the holiness of Heschel's earthly sojourn as a 'disclosure of the divine.' A truly important book; not to be missed."

—Beverly Lanzetta,
Theologian, Spiritual Teacher

"Harold Kasimow is one of the most creative and inspiring disciples of Abraham Joshua Heschel and, on the issue of religious diversity, he develops and goes beyond the pluralistic intuition of his master who claimed that 'in this eon diversity of religions is the will of God.' Kasimow not only writes meaningfully about other religions but he truly and sincerely encounters them at the deepest level. He is at home not only in his own Jewish tradition but also with the Buddhist, Hindu, Christian, and Muslim traditions—quite an unusual phenomenon in our polarized and conflicted world."

—Stanislaw Obirek,
American Studies Center, University of Warsaw

"Abraham Joshua Heschel's life and writings model a deep commitment to his own Jewish tradition, the depths of which enabled him to reach out, understand, and engage other faith traditions. He avoids both easy universalism and sectarian pride through his personal commitment to Torah, allowing him to set a model for others in a radical openness to other faiths that emerges from a Judaism that plumbs the depths to construct a broad and wide space for interreligious understanding and cooperation."

—John P. Keenan,
Professor Emeritus of Religion at Middlebury College

"Anyone who is interested in the powerful voice of Abraham Joshua Heschel will be interested in Harold Kasimow's book. *Interfaith Activism* is written by a scholar who had a personal relationship with Heschel. Heschel was Kasimow's teacher, mentor and friend, and remains the most important spiritual influence in his life. 'He is my hero,' Kasimow says. While Kasimow has written about Heschel for nearly 60 years, this book collects his published essays about Heschel over the last dozen years. Who could resist reading Kasimow's arrangement of Heschel's core ideas that focus on religious diversity as the will of God and on social activism as our way of implementing that will?"

—Kenneth P. Kramer,
Professor Emeritus of Religious Studies,
San Jose State University

"Harold Kasimow, with his ideal and intimate acquaintance with the whole of Heschel's thought, does not hesitate to touch upon difficult and disputed questions, such as Heschel's struggle with God's role during the Holocaust. He also highlights Heschel's unique contribution to the Catholic-Jewish dialogues that led to the Second Vatican Council's revolutionary document *Nostra Aetate*: Declaration on the Relationship of the Church to Non-Christian Religions."

—Shoshona Ronen,
Chair of Hebrew Studies at the Faculty of Oriental Studies,
Warsaw University

Interfaith Activism

Interfaith Activism

Abraham Joshua Heschel and Religious Diversity

Harold Kasimow

Forewords by
Edward Kaplan
Alan Race

and

Eboo Patel

WIPF & STOCK · Eugene, Oregon

INTERFAITH ACTIVISM
Abraham Joshua Heschel and Religious Diversity

Copyright © 2015 Harold Kasimow. All rights reserved. Except for brief quotations in critical publications or reviews, no part of this book may be reproduced in any manner without prior written permission from the publisher. Write: Permissions. Wipf and Stock Publishers, 199 W. 8th Ave., Suite 3, Eugene, OR 97401.

Wipf & Stock
An Imprint of Wipf and Stock Publishers
199 W. 8th Ave., Suite 3
Eugene, OR 97401

www.wipfandstock.com

ISBN 13: 978-1-4982-2479-6

Manufactured in the U.S.A.   01/28/2016

"Did Rabbi Heschel Influence Pope Francis" published in Interreligious Insight: A Journal of Dialogue and Engagement, 13:1 (June 2015). Reprinted with permission. An earlier version of this essay titled *"Interfaith Affinity: The Shared Vision of Rabbi Heschel and Pope Francis"* was originally published in *America* (October 27, 2014) and is reprinted with the permission of America Press, Inc., americanmagazine.org.

"Heschel's View of Religious Diversity" in *Studies in Christian-Jewish Relations*, 2 (2007), 19–25, and in *Abraham Joshua Heschel: Philosophy, Theology and Interreligious Dialogue*, edited by Stanislaw Krajewski and Adam Lipsyzc, (Wiesbaden: Harrassowitz Verlag, 2009). Reprinted with permission.

"Prophetic Voices: Abraham Joshua Heschel's Friendship with Martin Luther King, Jr." in *Interreligious Insight*, Vol. 7 (April 2009). Reprinted with permission.

"Rabbi Abraham Joshua Heschel's Paths to God" in *Maven in Blue Jeans: A Festschrift in Honor of Zev Garber*, Steven Leonard Jacobs, (West Lafayette, IN: Purdue University Press, 2009). Reprinted with permission.

"Spiritual Masters in the Jewish Tradition" in *Spiritual Masters in the World's Religions*, Arvind Sharma and Victoria Urubshurow, State University of New York Press, 2012. Reprinted with permission.

"Swami Vivekananda and Rabbi Abraham Joshua Heschel: Standing on the Shoulders of Giants" in *Interreligious Insight: A Journal of Dialogue and Engagement*, 1:3 (July 2003). Reprinted with permission.

"You Are My Witnesses: Maurice Friedman and Abraham Joshua Heschel" in *Dialogically Speaking: Maurice Friedman's Interdisciplinary Humanism*, ed. Kenneth Paul Kramer (Eugene: Pickwick Publications, 2011). Reprinted with permission.

To my dear friend John Merkle, Professor of Theology at the College of Saint Benedict and Saint John's University and the director of the Jay Phillips Center for Interfaith Learning in Minnesota. John, a leading Heschel scholar, has devoted his life to healing the rift between people of different faiths, especially Jews and Christians. John, who has a golden heart, has been a trusted friend for many decades.

Contents

Foreword by Edward K. Kaplan | ix
Foreword by Alan Race | xv
Foreword by Eboo Patel | xix
Acknowledgments | xxiii
Introduction | xxv

1 Rabbi Abraham Joshua Heschel's Path to God | 1
2 Heschel's View of Religious Diversity | 20
3 Spiritual Masters in the Jewish Tradition | 29
4 Abraham Joshua Heschel: Living with the Holocaust | 47
5 Swami Vivekananda and Rabbi Abraham Joshua Heschel: Standing on the Shoulders of Giants | 54
6 You Are My Witnesses: Maurice Friedman and Abraham Joshua Heschel | 64
7 Prophetic Voices: Abraham Joshua Heschel's Friendship with Martin Luther King Jr. | 75
8 Did Rabbi Heschel Influence Pope Francis? | 83

Bibliography | 95

Foreword

Edward Kaplan

HAROLD KASIMOW AND I inaugurated our spiritual and professional friendship under the aegis of interfaith scholarship on Abraham Joshua Heschel. We met in 1983 at the first conference on Heschel's life and works. That grounding-breaking symposium, at which so many other partnerships were forged, was organized by a young Catholic theologian, John C. Merkle, who had written his doctoral dissertation at the Catholic University of Louvain on Heschel's "depth theology," the genesis of faith in the living God. It is perhaps ironic that, after the pioneering work of Fritz A. Rothschild, Heschel scholarship was launched in earnest at a Catholic academic institution, the College of Saint Benedict in St. Joseph, Minnesota, to commemorate the tenth anniversary of Heschel's death.

At that conference we met some of Heschel's closest collaborators and friends: Samuel H. Dresner, a disciple from Heschel's earliest years in the United States; Heschel's dear friend Wolfe Kelman; Fritz Rothschild, a colleague from the Jewish Theological Seminary who was already Heschel's first major interpreter; Ursula Niebuhr, the widow of Reinhold, who promoted Heschel as a spiritual model of national stature; and many others. Merkle

Foreword by Edward Kaplan

published the proceedings in *Abraham Joshua Heschel: Exploring His Life and Thought*.

Thus, Harold and I had initiated a lifelong conversation. Fast forward to June 2007, when we participated in the first international conference on Heschel at the University of Warsaw, in the city where Heschel was born, organized by Stanislaw Krajewski and Adam Lipszyc and published as *Abraham Joshua Heschel: Philosophy, Theology and Interreligious Dialogue*. During that trip to Poland, we also visited Krakow, where Harold was honored for his numerous contributions to Polish-Jewish dialogue. The culmination was Harold's book, in Polish and English, *Poszukiwanie was wyzwoli. Judaizm w dialogu z religiami* świata; English: *The Search Will Make You Free: A Jewish Dialogue with World Religions*.

Harold Kasimow is a person of infinite gentleness. He conveys a deep reverence for all human beings, yet profoundly, with discretion, never denying the wounds of being Jewish. Harold is, above all, a loyal Jew dedicated to a prophetic vision of the ultimate reconciliation of peoples. His writings and teachings bear witness to the universal values of all religions—Christianity, Islam, Hinduism, Buddhism, and of course Judaism. But Harold the scholar does not speak in his own voice alone. The present book generously expresses gratitude to his teachers, especially to Maurice Friedman and Abraham Joshua Heschel.

Yet those "American" influences alone do not explain Harold's lifelong devotion to interfaith dialogue. He is among those courageous and sensitive souls for whom confronting the Holocaust opened his heart to others.

Kasimow gives his clearest self-portrait in the opening essay of *The Search Will Make You Free*, dedicated to the memory of Pope John Paul II.

> I was born in 1937 in a *shtetl*, a small village, not far from Vilnius, Lithuania, which at that time was part of Poland. On July 2, 1941, just before my fourth birthday, the German army took control of our village. We lived under a traumatizing German occupation until April 3, 1942, when a priest informed my father of a massacre of the

Foreword by Edward Kaplan

Jews in Braslau, a nearby village. This was our last chance to escape, and we did.

For the next several months my parents, my two older sisters, and I hid in barns and attics and many other places, helped by farmers in this area who risked their lives to help us. When we all became sick with horrible coughs and could no longer hide near any home, my father dug a deep ditch in the forest, where we stayed for five weeks.

This objective account suggests how Harold Kasimow, as a child, pursued by the murderers, made a decisive existential step into compassion. The heroism of their decent non-Jewish acquaintances confirmed the boy's belief in the goodness of a great many Polish people and, by extension, of all people:

For the last nineteen months and five days before the war ended, my father excavated a tunnel beneath a stall in a barn that was next to the house of Wladislaw Piworowitz, a farmer he knew. We shared our underground hideout with mice, frogs, and worms. We also dug a small hole for defecation and urination. The entire time we were in the dark and did not wash. We were all infected with lice.

Throughout the war we lived in constant fear of being discovered by the Nazis or others who would turn us in to the Nazis. On a number of occasions my family and I came very close to being found. Nearly all my relatives, including my mother's mother, with whom I had a special relationship, were murdered during the Holocaust.

It is impossible for those of us who have not experienced these horrors (so realistically, though diffidently evoked) to fathom not only how Harold Kasimow survived mentally—to understand how he did not succumb to bitterness or to despair—but also to grasp how compassion became a ruling value of his life.

The next paragraph of this spiritual autobiography appears, at first, to effect a brusque transition. How could unconscionable trauma, which might enslave him to the past, lead to faith in an ethical future?

Foreword by Edward Kaplan

> These early experiences profoundly affected my life, which I have devoted to the study of the major religions of the world. I have been particularly attracted to saints, spiritual men and women of great compassion who are not preoccupied with themselves but with the suffering of other people, and who never adjust to violence but are free of it; they dedicate their lives to bringing compassion to the people of our planet. I have been fortunate to meet a number of such extraordinary men and women from different religious traditions. They have had a great impact on me.

As a scholar Harold Kasimow chose to explore the mysteries of human compassion rather than dwelling upon the motives and methods of the Nazi murderers and their "willing executioners" (in Daniel Jonah Goldhagen's phrase). Harold made a profound existential decision. After the war, growing from his identification with Lithuanian Judaism, he absorbed the Musar tradition established by Rabbi Israel Salanter (1810–1883) in Vilnius in the 1840s. This provided the new American that Harold had become with a Jewish spiritual discipline: "[Salanter] devoted his life to guiding Jews on the path to ethical perfection, to the transformation of the individual." This helps explain how Harold's study of saints became a foundation of interfaith dialogue. All religious traditions revere ethical perfection in one form or another.

One of the most valuable contributions of this new book is the chapter "Spiritual Masters in the Jewish Tradition." As he explains:

> I was born a few years before the Nazi occupation in a small village near Vilna in a traditional Orthodox Jewish family, although my mother's family belonged to the Lakhovich-Koidanov Hasidic dynasties of Lithuania. My education was also very traditional. When I arrived with my family in the United States after the war, I studied at Yeshiva Salanter, and then at Talmudical Academy of Yeshiva University. My Jewish education continued at the Jewish Theological Seminary and at the University of Jerusalem. Today, after nearly thirty-five years of study

Foreword by Edward Kaplan

of other religious traditions and having participated in a number of meditation retreats under the direction of Zen Buddhist masters in the U.S., Canada, and Japan, I believe that I have developed a deeper understanding of and attachment to my own tradition. Although I consider myself to be a committed Jew, I am also a pluralist deeply influenced by both Friedman and Heschel.

Harold Kasimow's lifetime of reflection on spiritual integrity allowed him to include in his pantheon not only Moses Hayyim Luzzatto (1707–1746) and Rabbi Israel Salanter, along with Heschel and his thesis adviser Maurice Friedman, but also the Dalai Lama, Pope John Paul II, Swami Vivekananda, Martin Luther King Jr., and Pope Francis. Readers and practitioners can enter Harold's community of interfaith scholars in his collection of essays co-edited with Byron L. Sherwin (of blessed memory), *No Religion Is an Island: Abraham Joshua Heschel and Interreligious Dialogue*. Harold Kasimow takes his rightful place among representatives of Jewish, Catholic, Protestant, Hindu, Buddhist, and Muslim traditions.

The present book provides a most lucid introduction to the works of Rabbi Abraham Joshua Heschel, whose open-minded and mystical Judaism provides—in Kasimow's deft interpretations—reasons to hope that are both empirical and holy.

Foreword

Alan Race

ABRAHAM JOSHUA HESCHEL IS celebrated in Harold Kasimow's book as a "beloved teacher" par excellence, and without doubt an inspiration serving a purpose wider even than many good teachers might manage. Heschel's torch burns brightly in the hands of this devoted student and interpreter, one who is keen on communicating his legacy and whose own instincts are equally expansive and wedded to truthfulness for our time. If Judaism down the ages has known many heroes of Jewish conviction and life, then Harold Kasimow positions Heschel with distinguished company. "Saint" may not be a common Jewish category but Kasimow is not shy of claiming the epithet for one of Judaism's modern heroes.

To be in the company of Abraham Heschel is to be in the company of one of the twentieth century's best religious minds. I say 'religious' because, although Heschel was first and foremost a devoted follower of Torah and Judaism, his instincts reached well beyond the boundaries of that single tradition. Both his heart and his head refused to be hemmed in. For that reason alone he remains a prophet not only of the twentieth century but also of the twenty-first, which still remains suspicious of too much rapprochement between cultures, religions, and traditions, and which is unnervingly witness to a rise in so-called religiously-motivated violence. To be sure, there are many calls for collaboration and dialogue across boundaries, but many remain ambivalent about such endeavors. The intellectual explorations of difference combined with a fearless compassion for a just and loving world is Heschel's legacy, one which the twenty-first century could do with heeding above all else. This collection of reflections on Heschel's theological achievements by Harold Kasimow, a persistent admirer of the master, serves to keep that legacy forcefully alive.

Writing this foreword sent me back to Heschel's remarkable lecture, "No Religion Is an Island," given at Union Theological Seminary, New York, in 1965. It reads even now as a rallying cry fit for a globalizing world. In the background is the unimaginable horror of the Holocaust, in the foreground the need to establish dialogical commitments fit for an emerging post-Holocaust world. There is the epistemological reckoning too in Heschel's wrestling with the concept of God's hidden transcendence in relation to the frail earthenware vessels that are the world's religious traditions. The whole lecture is remarkable for its open generosity of spirit while remaining resolute in the face of the world's evils. It must have been both thrilling and unsettling to the ears of its first hearers.

The Hebrew Scriptures were Heschel's first love. But the scriptures are not a museum or curiosity shop for voyeurs; they are for living with and living through. From them, and especially the prophetic books, Heschel forged ideas such as the "pathos of God," a highly suggestive if not altogether orthodox notion, for a twentieth century longing to articulate a belief in divine responsiveness to human suffering in the face of what many saw as divine indifference in a world of untold suffering. The "pathos of God" would resonate too with Christian reflections of the same period, wondering how God relates to a world characterized by self-sufficiency yet simultaneously aware of the anxiety which accompanies feelings of abandonment in an unfeeling universe.

For Heschel, the Hebrew Scriptures were unsurpassable among the world's religious treasures, yet he sought to combine this foundational affirmation with an equal and comparable stress on other religious traditions as effective vehicles for conveying humanity toward God. For those religious philosophers who push as hard as possible for a high degree of internal consistency in theological argumentation, there may be an unresolved tension here in the relationship between the belief in Hebrew Scripture's unsurpassability and the equal stress on an equality of effectiveness among other traditions. If there is an equality of effectiveness, how does this square with the Bible's unsurpassable, and thereby superior, status? Be that as it may, it does not detract from Heschel's overall purpose, which was never to limit the divine reaching out to the world, thereby maximizing the divine embrace of creation.

Part of the impact of the concept of hero is that heroes yield a legacy which continues to have dynamic meaning. So Kasimow brings out clearly how Heschel's work and life extended in numerous directions, especially into Christian consciousness. Most notable in this regard was Heschel's advocacy for the recognition of Jewish authenticity in the document *Nostra Aetate*, one of the seminal products emanating from Vatican II, that bold Catholic turning to the world at a time of immense social and political change. That *Nostra Aetate* signaled the end of Christian supersessionism over Judaism was due in large part to the representation that Heschel made to that great Council.

A second lasting significance of Heschel was his relationship with Martin Luther King Jr. in the struggles over civil rights in America in the 1960s. The two became deep friends and companions in theology as well as in social activism. Moreover, social justice represents an indivisible demand and therefore must be applied wherever there is need. This, of course, is all of a piece with Heschel's deep commitment to the insights of the Hebrew prophets. Heschel was no ivory tower philosopher.

Thirdly, and bringing the trajectory of Heschel's influence up to date, it might well be that his wisdom has been a subtle influence on Pope Francis, in so far as the two men share the common spirituality that God is present to all humanity and craves for their total well-being. As Kasimow indicates, there is more than enough material in these shared perceptions of divine universal presence for a dialogue between religions, which in turn would contribute to reversing much of the religious antagonism inherited from a fractured and fractious past.

In fact, Kasimow had already pointed out the advantages of engaging with Abraham Heschel in his earlier book, *Divine-Human Encounter: A Study of Abraham Joshua Heschel* (1979), which was based on his PhD thesis. It is likely that this book was the first book to point out how Heschel's thought might contribute to a productive dialogue between Jews and Christians, and indeed between Jews and the more "mystic" worlds of Asian traditions. The book also brought our attention to Heschel's belief that Judaism, in turn, might itself be enriched through a dialogue "between the river Jordan and the river Ganges." For it to be effective dialogue is necessarily a two-way street, a "mutual irradiation" as it has been called, both sides being prepared to learn something new from the other.

The essential ingredients of Heschel's thought remain as relevant today as they were pertinent in the mid-twentieth century, and in many respects more so. So, theological problems concerning the nature of God's relationship with the world (the pathos of God) are perennial and even more pressing today with the realization that secular models of explanation for human experience are as limited as are many religious proposals. Then, issues of social justice and reconciliation between ethnic and cultural groups take new forms and create new challenges with each succeeding generation. Finally, the challenges of interfaith dialogue and the theological interpretation of religious pluralism have assumed center stage for many in both the academy and the faith communities.

Harold Kasimow has performed a great service for us by highlighting these problems in Heschel's work and life and thus demonstrating his continuing relevance for a confusing world, which is shaped by all the globalizing forces we are challenged by as twenty-first century human beings.

Foreword

Eboo Patel

My mother had a friend, a senior colleague at the community college where she teaches, a man who had adventured in countries I'd never even heard of and who had somehow settled down in the western suburbs of Chicago. Marvin was an American aquarium drinker; a man who contained multitudes. He would order off the Chinese language menu at Argyle Street eateries, he knew when the chicken was fresh at the restaurant owned by Moroccan Jews on Devon Avenue, he would take the widow of the Consul General of the Philippines to the Walnut Room at Marshall Fields on State Street every Christmas holiday. When Marvin learned that my wife was a civil rights attorney, he began spontaneously quoting Clarence Darrow courtroom speeches at remarkable length. I can't even tell you how many religious passages he photocopied for me, placing them in manila folders and putting them in my hands with the line, "This'll give you something to think about."

I seriously believed that Marvin had so much life that death would turn and run. But that's not how this world works. Toward the end, when I would visit him in Evanston hospital, he didn't regale me with the thousand things he was expert on—no chit chat about online poker or presidential wills. Marvin had only one subject at that stage, one focus. He would pull me so close I could smell old age on his skin and he would say, "Have you been reading Heschel?"

Abraham Joshua Heschel. In his last days, that was Marvin's only topic of conversation with me. I'd heard of Heschel before, here and there, but never paid him much mind. Yet the way Marvin breathed the name—like a wish, like a will, like a prayer—there on his deathbed.... Well, I went out and bought some Heschel.

And as I read, I felt like the angels had descended and were singing around me, like I was in a room surrounded by Chagall Windows and the characters were dancing. It is writing that brings the light of heaven to the Harlem of life. It is writing that reminds me why I am a Muslim, and this is not just because Rabbi Heschel sports a bushy beard.

What first moved me about Islam, after a long time with my back turned to the tradition, was the sense that we are put here by the Source for big things. The Qur'an says, "God did not create the Heavens and the earth and what is between them in sport." God gave humankind a mission to fulfill; God believes in us.

In Islam, we are taught that God picks up a lump of clay and gives it His breath and thereby creates Adam, the first human being, the representative of all humankind. God tells Adam that he was made to be His abd and Khalifa, his servant and representative upon the earth. The Angels are called forth and God tells them to bow to the figure he has entrusted with His Creation. The Angels are petulant. Why shall we honor a creature who will only fiddle and destroy, they ask.

"I know what you do not know," God responds.

Allah then sets up a contest between Adam and the Angels. He asks the Angels to name the different parts of Creation. The Angels reply that the only knowledge they have is to sing of God's glory.

God gives the same task to Adam, but first He gives Adam a treasure—the ability to name the names of Creation. Adam wins the contest.

There was a very small detail in that Qur'annic verse that focused my attention: the word names. Adam needs to learn many names. He is not to just repeat the same name over and over. The Angels do not know many names. They only know one name—the name of God's glory. But Creation is not just one thing. Creation is many things. Creation is diverse. Adam is to be God's servant and representative in this environment. Adam needs to learn to flow in diversity.

It is a story that has great resonance in Abraham Joshua Heschel's work. "Man's most precious thought is God," he says, "but God's most precious thought is man. . . . [We are] holy of holies."

In the Qur'an, when the Angels scorn Adam, God's response is: "I know what you do not know."

Think what this means. God vouches for our goodness to the Angels. God is convinced that we are worthy to be His vicegerent. Heschel put it this way: "We are God's stake in human history, regardless of merit and often against our will."

Heschel's central question is the same as the central question of the Qur'an: Will we live up to the task that God put before us? And the quality that God gives us that distinguishes us from the Angels, the quality that marks us as God's abd and Khalifa, that will allow us to live up to this task is speech. This is a core theme in Heschel's writing. "Speech has power," he says. "Words do not fade. What begins in a word, ends in a deed."

The Holocaust, Heschel reminds us, did not begin with concentration camps. It began with language. And the horror of the Holocaust was not about God forsaking humankind, but God waiting and longing for human beings to live up to His expectations of us. "God is waiting for us to redeem the world," Heschel writes.

What is that task? How are we to redeem the world? The answer is stunningly simple, although the application is exceedingly difficult. It is to love truth and do mercy. Heschel loved to say that the great joy of the psalmist is that truth and mercy are together. He wrote, "A religious man is a person who holds God and man in one thought at one time, at all times, who suffers in himself the harm done to others, whose greatest passion is compassion, whose greatest strength is love and defiance of despair."

In Islam, truth is clear. There is one God and Muhammad is his messenger. And in Islam, mercy is central; it is what the Creator of truth demands of his most precious creation—humankind. The first lesson that classical Muslim scholars would teach their students is this: "If you are merciful to those on earth, the One who is in heaven will be merciful to you." The Qur'an says that the Prophet Muhammad, may the peace and blessings of God be upon him, was sent as nothing but a special mercy upon all the worlds. There are Muslim scholars who say that the entire Qur'an needs to be read in the light of the one central value—mercy.

Heschel celebrated his tradition as a source of beauty and exaltation. But he critiqued it as well, and as I read that critique of contemporary Judaism I thought to myself, "This could just as easily be said about present-day Islam." Heschel writes: "The trouble is that some see all of Judaism reflected in its Law; in their concern for the letter of the Law they give up the Jewish spark. They make the fence more important than the tradition it is meant to protect. Such extremism and severity do us great harm; even the Creator of the world, finding that a world could not exist by justice alone, combined the quality of justice with the quality of mercy."

Why do I see Islam so intimately refracted in Heschel's work? I believe that Heschel understood the holiness of diversity as well as anyone. Different religions are part of that diversity and have a special responsibility to cherish and protect it. To accomplish this task, we need to work together.

Acknowledgments

ABRAHAM JOSHUA HESCHEL OFTEN spoke of the centrality of gratitude as a basic response to the wonder of human life. In this spirit, I would like to express my own deepest thanks to the many people who helped me with this book of essays. First and foremost, I gladly acknowledge my beloved teacher, Dr. Heschel, who helped me to see the beauty of the Jewish tradition but at the same time to discern the spiritual riches within other religious traditions. Heartfelt gratitude goes to my teacher Maurice Friedman, of blessed memory, who many years ago encouraged me to write my PhD thesis on Heschel. I would also like to express my deepest gratitude to Rabbi Byron Sherwin, Heschel's most insightful disciple, for his many years of friendship. May his memory be for a blessing.

I am particularly honored that Edward Kaplan, Alan Race, and Eboo Patel, three distinguished religious voices of our time, found the time to write forewords for this book.

Very important to me has been the friendship and tremendous support of William Burrows, Zev Garber, John Keenan, Linda Keenan, Kenneth Kramer, Beverly Lanzetta, Stanislaw Obirek, Alan Race, and Jacob Yuroh Teshima. I am especially grateful to George A. Drake, former president of Grinnell College, for his interest in my work and for his continuing encouragement and to my students at Grinnell College, who for four decades helped me

Acknowledgments

to deepen my understanding of Heschel's complex thought. In the words of Rabbi Hanina, "I have learned much from my teachers, more from my colleagues, but most from my students."

I am profoundly grateful to Russ Tabbert for his talented editorial skills. It is always a great joy to work with Angela Winburn a dear friend and co-worker at Grinnell College who worked with great diligence to ensure an accurate typescript.

I would like to thank the editorial staff at Wipf and Stock, especially Matthew Wimer and Brian Palmer.

I would also like to thank my wife Lolya Lipchitz and my daughters Sophie and Johanna Kasimow for their encouragement and understanding.

Heschel and Jacob Teshima, November 1971,
courtesy of Jacob Yuroh Teshima

Introduction

ONE OF THE GREATEST blessings in my life was having the opportunity to study with Rabbi Abraham Joshua Heschel (1907–1972), may his memory be for a blessing. After I graduated from Yeshiva University High School in New York City in 1956, I enrolled at The Seminary College of Jewish Studies of The Jewish Theological Seminary of America, also in New York City, where Heschel was my adviser. In the 1957–1958 academic year I took two courses with him. One was a course in the philosophy of religion, in which the main text was his classic work *God in Search of Man: A Philosophy of Judaism*. The other was on Genesis, with an emphasis on Rashi's interpretation. Rashi, an acronym for Rabbi Shlomo Yetzhaki (1040–1105), is the most important Jewish commentator on the Bible and Talmud. According to Heschel, Rashi democratized Jewish education. Our class of about ten students included some rabbinical students. Heschel was not happy with the fact that even some of them didn't know Rashi well. For that reason we went very slowly. For homework he would assign a section of Genesis with Rashi's interpretation. Because I was so taken by Heschel, I would stay up all night preparing for the class. I distinctly remember one day when he called on me and I responded well. Afterwards, I danced all the way from the seminary on 121st Street and Broadway to 161st Street where I lived.

Introduction

I graduated from the seminary college with a Bachelor of Hebrew Literature in 1961. From 1961 to 1963, I served in the Army working in military education in Okinawa and Thailand. This presented me with a wonderful opportunity to spend time with Buddhist monks, which clearly influenced my fascination with Buddhism. I have continued to study and teach Buddhism to the present day. In 1963, after being discharged from the Army, I was fortunate to attend a lecture given by Professor Heschel in the Boston area. I met with him after his talk and was thrilled that he still remembered me by name.

In 1967, Heschel wrote a recommendation for me when I applied to graduate school in the department of religion at Temple University. One day, while visiting Professor Bernard Phillips, the department's founder and chairman, I asked him about my application for his graduate program. In the ensuing conversation, I discovered that he had only received two letters of recommendation for me. At first I was concerned because I knew that he needed three such letters. "Don't worry," Phillips said to me. "One of your letters of recommendation is from Abraham Joshua Heschel and, that being the case, you don't need another letter." Here again, Heschel played a major role on my road to my PhD and my academic life.

In 1971–72, while preparing for my PhD dissertation on Heschel, I traveled from Philadelphia to New York City once a week to take the seminar that he was teaching to his rabbinical students on his book *Torah min-HaShamayim*. After class I spent many hours with him in his office discussing possible topics for my thesis. At that point, I was quite fluent in Yiddish and Hebrew, and he gave me a number of his articles in these languages. Later in the day I would walk him home before returning to Philadelphia.

The last time I saw Heschel was June 13, 1972. He read the proposal for my dissertation and wrote "a fine outline, a good promise," which I showed to my advisers. That, of course, gave me great confidence, encouragement, and strength to move forward. I told him that I had accepted a position at Grinnell College in Iowa and he seemed pleased with my decision, perhaps because he had

Introduction

been a visiting professor at the nearby University of Iowa where he was treated with a great deal of affection and respect.

The last time I spoke to Heschel was only two weeks later, on Friday, June 30, 1972. He called me to give me his address in Los Angeles, California, where he was going for the rest of the summer. I was pleasantly surprised by the call, imagining that he called so that I could reach him if I needed some help. Sadly, he died on December 23, 1972. I never had a chance to talk to him about my Grinnell experience nor my dissertation on his understanding of the divine-human encounter.

When my dissertation was eventually published in 1979 as *Divine-Human Encounter: A Study of Abraham Joshua Heschel*, Maurice Friedman, one of Heschel's great friends and my principal dissertation adviser, wrote in the foreword to the book, "I myself spoke with Professor Heschel several times about the work that Professor Kasimow was doing on his thought. Heschel was pleased with it because Kasimow brought a full knowledge of Heschel's Hebrew and Yiddish writings as well as his English and German ones." Professor Friedman's words pleased me greatly, as did a letter I received from Mrs. Heschel on July 24, 1979, soon after the book was published, in which she wrote, "To my pleasure I found it interesting and a real contribution. It is a fair study, carefully planned and definitely a contribution for those who do not know all aspects of Dr. Heschel's writings." I was especially delighted when Mrs. Heschel came to see me in Boston on July 7, 1987, and wrote the following in my favorite Heschel book, *Man Is Not Alone*: "To Professor Kasimow, whose discernment, scholarly appraisals, and honesty I respect, as I know my husband would."

More than anything else, what had drawn me to Heschel was his stress on the ethical dimension of Judaism, which aims at ethical perfection, the total transformation of the human being. It is an emphasis on *aggadah*, that is, spirituality, not just on *halakhah*, which is law. In *aggadah* the focus is on what is in the heart of the believer while he or she fulfills the demands of God, not only on the doing of the deed itself. Heschel believed that one of the goals of Judaism is to create a harmony between *halakhah* and

Introduction

aggadah. For him, the ethical aspect of Judaism is as important as the ritualistic. I still have the notes from my last course with Heschel. For example, on October 14, 1971, he said that there is a tradition that Judaism has no theology. For fifteen hundred years, the primary emphasis was placed on *halakhah*. When one comes to *aggadah* that section was skipped. Heschel said that we do have a Jewish theology; *aggadah* is theology. The Talmudic rabbis were concerned with theological issues. You cannot solve, he said, all problems with *halakhah* alone. In Psalms there is no *halakhah*. Most of the Bible is *aggadah*.

Heschel also believed that a pious person has to be as mindful of relations with other human beings as of the relationship with God. According to Heschel, we must be "alert to the dignity of every human being." He writes that the pious person is "keenly sensitive to pain and suffering in our own life and in that of others." In his book on the Jews of Eastern Europe, *The Earth Is the Lord's*, Heschel gives the following definition of a saint: "A saint was he who did not know how it is possible not to love, not to help, not to be sensitive to the anxiety of others."

Today, with tensions among Jews, Christians, and Muslims at painful and dangerous levels, dialogue is imperative. Heschel stated "history has made us all neighbors. The age of moral mediocrity and complacency has run out. This is a time for radical commitment, for radical action." Many people from different religious traditions have been drawn to Heschel's message of hope. No other Jewish thinker, that I know, has shown more love for God and God's creation and optimism for the potential of humanity to mirror the love of God.

How fortunate, no, how blessed, I am to have had such a close personal relationship with Rabbi Heschel. I have been studying and writing about his thought for nearly sixty years. He was a superlative teacher and remains the most important spiritual influence in my life. He is my hero. This book collects my essays about him and his thought published over the last dozen years.

The focus of the first essay, "Rabbi Abraham Joshua Heschel's Path to God," is on the interrelated, three-fold path to encounter

Introduction

God, which is best developed in Heschel's major work *God in Search of Man*. The essay also explores Heschel's central, controversial doctrine of divine pathos, his claim that whatever we do affects not only us but also God.

The fact of religious diversity has been the big question for me, even before I studied with Heschel. What exactly does Heschel mean when he states that "in this aeon diversity of religions is the will of God"? I have devoted a great deal of time to this issue, beginning with my essay "Abraham Joshua Heschel and Interreligious Dialogue," first published in the *Journal of Ecumenical Studies* in 1981. Here the second essay gives my current understanding of Heschel's view on this critical issue.

The third essay, "Jewish Spiritual Masters," compares and contrasts the path to holiness developed by Moses Hayyim Luzzatto (1707–1746) in his book *The Path of the Upright* with the path to holiness that Heschel develops in *God in Search of Man*. Luzzatto was the most important Jewish mystic and ethicist of the eighteenth century, while in my view Heschel was the most authentic Jewish mystic and ethicist of the twentieth.

In the fourth essay, I explore the profound impact that the Holocaust had on Heschel's life and thought. This essay can be seen as a response to those who have criticized Heschel for not allowing the Holocaust to influence his writings. Certainly Heschel did not want to put the Holocaust at the center of Judaism, which belongs to Sinai. But there should be no doubt that his involvements in the Civil Rights Movement, the Second Vatican Council's discussions about interfaith relations, and other social and political issues were in large measure due not only to his study of the prophets but also to his Holocaust experience.

In the fifth essay, "Swami Vivekananda and Rabbi Abraham Joshua Heschel: Standing on the Shoulders of Giants," which I see as my most unique essay, I attempt to capture the affinity between Swami Vivekananda (1863–1902), the charismatic Hindu monist, and Rabbi Heschel (1907–1972), the Jewish theist, on a number of significant religious issues including their views of other religious traditions.

Introduction

The next two essays examine the great friendship and theological compatibility that Heschel had with Martin Luther King Jr. and with Maurice Friedman, the brilliant Buber scholar who considered himself to be a "near disciple" of Heschel.

The final essay, written with my dear friend John Merkle, develops the surprisingly strong affinity between Pope Francis and Rabbi Heschel on many critical issues, including the urgency of dialogue.

I invite readers interested in Heschel's provocative work to especially read and ponder the following four sentences:

- *The world is too small for anything but mutual care and deep respect; the world is too great for anything but responsibility for one another.*

- *We must insist upon loyalty to the unique and holy treasures of our own tradition and at the same time acknowledge that in this aeon religious diversity may be a providence of God.*

- *To be human is to be involved, to act, and to react; to wonder and to respond.*

- *I've learned from the prophets that I have to be involved in the affairs of man, in the affairs of suffering man.*

These words, from the powerful voice of Abraham Joshua Heschel capture the core ideas in this collection of essays which focus on religious diversity as the will of God and on social activism as our way of implementing that will.

1

Rabbi Abraham Joshua Heschel's Path to God

IN HIS BEST KNOWN work, *God in Search of Man*—a book that has been called "the single most sophisticated, profound, and comprehensive statement within modern Judaic theology"[1]—Abraham Joshua Heschel, one of the most significant Jewish thinkers of the twentieth century, expresses his deep concern over the decline of religion today. This concern extends beyond the survival of Judaism to the survival of humanity itself. In a 1967 article he says:

> The cardinal problem is not the survival of religion, but the survival of man. What is required is a continuous effort to overcome hardness of heart, callousness, and above all to inspire the world with the Biblical image of man, not to forget that man without God is a torso, to prevent the dehumanization of man. For the opposite of human is not the animal. The opposite of the human is the demonic.[2]

It is with this prospect (essentially, the destruction of humanity) in mind that Heschel says, "The most serious problem is the absence of the problem."[3] What he meant was that the modern

---

1. Neusner, *American Judaism*, 156.
2. Heschel, "What We Might Do Together," 135.
3. Heschel, *God in Search of Man*, 168. Cited hereafter as *GSM*.

1

world has been so taken over by atheism, agnosticism, and indifference to religion that most people don't even recognize that the absence of God in their lives is actually an issue.

From the first paragraph of *God in Search of Man*, Heschel seeks to examine the causes for the modern-day decline of religion. He starts with a provocative thesis. The central cause for the decline, he says, is not the rise of rationalism or secularism. The central cause lies within religion itself.

> Religion declined not because it was refuted, but because it became irrelevant, dull, oppressive, insipid. When faith is completely replaced by creed, worship by discipline, love by habit; . . . when religion speaks only in the name of authority rather than with the voice of compassion—its message becomes meaningless. (*GSM* 3)

But Heschel acknowledges that the rationalistic and scientific worldview prevalent today is partly responsible for the disappearance of faith.

> It is characteristic of the inner situation of contemporary man that the plausible way to identify himself is to see himself in the image of a machine. . . . Man is simply "a machine into which we put what we call food and produce what we call thought." The definition itself goes back to the eighteenth century. Never before, however, has it been so widely accepted as plausible.[4]

As the rationalistic-scientific worldview becomes more sophisticated it becomes more deeply materialistic. In a materialistic society our sense of immediacy begins to dominate more and more, while our sense of transcendence diminishes considerably.

When the exponents of reason went so far as to proclaim reason to be the only guide to truth, they in effect were saying that there was no longer any mystery that the human mind could not penetrate. "Whatever there is to know, that we shall know someday" (*GSM* 34). When reason became the be-all and end-all, revelation became unnecessary.

---

4. Heschel, *Who is Man?*, 23–24. Cited hereafter as *WM*.

Eighteenth-century thinkers attempted to harmonize reason and revelation by making revelation subject to the laws of reason, but they only made religion more irrelevant. As Heschel notes, "If science and religion are intrinsically identical, one of them must be superfluous. In such reconciliation religion is little more than bad science and naïve morality" (*GSM* 13). This opened the way for widespread atheism, agnosticism, and indifference to religion.

The rise in rationalism meant, in effect, that humanity no longer needed God. But starting with his dissertation in 1933, Heschel made a highly original contribution to Biblical thought: he asserted that not only do we need God, but God needs us. For Heschel, God is a God of pathos who suffers when we suffer. Alongside God's actions affecting us, our actions affect God. Heschel finds evidence for his highly controversial claim in scripture. "In all their affliction he was afflicted" (Isa 63:9). Also, "For a long time I have kept silent. I have kept still and restrained Myself; Now I will cry out like a woman in travail, I will gasp and pant" (Isa 42:14).

Heschel brings in passages from other Jewish sources:

> When Israel performs the will of the Omnipresent, they add strength to the heavenly power; as it is said, "To God we render strength!" When, however, Israel does not perform the will of the Omnipresent, they weaken—if it is possible to say so—the great power of Him who is above; as it is written "Thou didst weaken the Rock that begot thee" (Deut. 32:18).
>
> The Holy One, as it were, said: "When Israel is worthy below, My power prevails in the universe; but when Israel is found to be unworthy, she weakens my power above" (The Zohar).[5]

To provide a practical guide for how the modern mind can open itself to God, or more precisely, through which the contemporary mind can respond to a God who is in search of human beings, Heschel illustrated three paths to God in his seminal work, *God in Search of Man*:

---

5. Heschel, "The Mystical Element," 604–5.

> There are three starting points of contemplation about God; three trails that lead to him. The first is the way of sensing the presence of God in the world, in things; the second is the way of sensing His presence in the Bible; the third is the way of sensing His presence in sacred deeds (*GSM* 31).

Most of Heschel's other major works are primarily devoted to one of these three ways, or paths. *Man is Not Alone* is concerned with the first path, the way to God via the world, whereas *The Prophets* and *Heavenly Torah: As Refracted through the Generations* are devoted to the second, the way to God through the Bible. Heschel's "Man's Quest for God" is largely given to the third path, the way to God through sacred deeds.

The path to God through the world

To sense the presence of God in the world, modern humanity must do something quite radical. We must transform the way we view the world around us. We must part with the Greek philosophers who have become our guides and immerse ourselves in the viewpoint of Biblical men and women. According to Heschel:

> There are three aspects of nature that command our attention: its power, its beauty and its grandeur. Accordingly there are three ways in which we may relate ourselves to the world—we may exploit, we may enjoy it, we may accept it in awe" (*GSM* 33–34).

But the modern mind, writes Heschel, understands only the power of nature, and responds with a desire to control and exploit nature (*GSM* 34). The Biblical mind, on the other hand, was enchanted by the grandeur of nature, and responded with a sense of awe and wonder.

Fritz Rothschild, a specialist on Heschel's thought, writes:

> To recover the sensitivity to that dimension of reality which engenders wonder and worship Heschel turns to the experience of religious men and the classical

document of such experience, the Bible. There he finds six terms that describe grandeur and man's reaction to it in three correlative pairs: the sublime and wonder, mystery and awe, the glory and faith. It must be borne in mind that in each of these three pairs of terms the first one refers to an objective aspect of reality and the second one to man's mode of responding to it. All these terms refer to the realm of the ineffable.[6]

Heschel illustrates the first pair of terms, "sublime" and "wonder":

> The sublime is that which we see and are unable to convey. It is the silent allusion of things to a meaning greater than themselves. . . . It may be sensed in every grain of sand, in every drop of water. Every flower in the summer, every snowflake in the winter, may arouse in us the sense of wonder that is our response to the sublime (*GSM* 39).

This is a most crucial idea in Heschel's thought, for Heschel himself states, "Awareness of the divine begins with wonder" (*GSM* 56). Wonder is the fundamental attitude of the truly pious person.

To explain the word mystery Heschel turns to Wisdom literature. According to Heschel, there was nothing that did not hold a great secret for the Biblical mind. "What stirred their soul was neither the hidden nor the apparent, but the hidden in the apparent; not the order but the mystery of the order that prevails in the universe" (*GSM* 56). Just as a pious person cannot exist without the sense for the sublime, a pious person cannot exist without the sense of mystery. Heschel writes: "[T]he root of worship lies in the sense of the 'miracles that are daily with us.' There is neither worship nor ritual without a sense of mystery" (*GSM* 62).

Heschel explains that Biblical men and women did not respond to the mystery with a sense of resignation, with fear or terror, but with awe. "Awe . . . is the sense of wonder and humility inspired by the sublime or felt in the presence of mystery" (*GSM* 62). He argues that just as there is no faith without wonder, there

---

6. Rothschild, *Between God and Man*, 11.

is no faith without awe, explaining "We must grow in awe in order to reach faith" (*GSM* 77).

After examining "mystery" and "awe," Heschel turns to the third pair of terms and discusses one of the central concepts in Judaism, the "glory" of God. Here his thought takes up the ancient dynamic between two concepts found in Biblical literature: the transcendence of God and the immanence of God. According to some scholars, Judaism has suffered from an undue stress on God's transcendence and neglected God's immanence. But Heschel turns to the book of Isaiah to show us the coexistence of the two concepts:

> In his great vision Isaiah perceives the voice of the seraphim even before he hears the voice of the Lord. What is it that the seraphim reveal? "Holy, holy, holy is the Lord of Hosts; the whole earth is full of his Glory." "Holy, holy, holy"—indicates the transcendence and distance of God. "The whole earth is full of his Glory"—the immanence or presence of God (*GSM* 89).

As Professor Israel Efros explains, "Holiness tries to lift the God-idea ever above the expanding corporeal universe, and Glory tends to bring the Creator ever nearer to man."[7]

Heschel describes what the Glory of God means for humanity:

> Standing face to face with the world, we often sense a presence which surpasses our ability to comprehend. The world is too much for us. It is crammed with marvel. There is a glory, an aura, that lies about all beings, a spiritual setting of reality (*WM* 90).

According to Heschel, we are citizens in two realms.

> The tangible phenomena we scrutinize with our reason, the sacred and indemonstrable we overhear with the sense of the ineffable. The force that inspires readiness for self-sacrifice, the thoughts that breed humility within and beyond the mind, are not identical with the logician's craftsmanship. The purity of which we never cease

---

7. Efros, *Ancient Jewish Philosophy*, 7.

to dream, the untold things we insatiably love, the vision of the good for which we either die or perish alive—no reason can bound. It is the ineffable from which we draw the taste of the sacred, the joy of the imperishable.[8]

Heschel says the possibility of experiencing the Glory is not closed to contemporary humanity. We are certainly capable of responding with wonder and radical amazement to the grandeur and the sublime. We are capable of responding with awe to the mystery, with faith to the glory. Why then do we so often fail? We fail, says Heschel, because of indifference:

> This is the tragedy of every man, "to dim all wonder by indifference." Life is routine, and routine is resistance to wonder . . . said the Baal Shem[,] "Just as a small coin held over the face can block out the sight of the mountain, so the vanities of the living block out the sight of the infinite light" (*GSM* 85).

But even if we are able to overcome our indifference and react to God's presence with a sense of awe and wonder, we have not yet completed our journey to God, says Heschel.

> "It is not a feeling for the mystery of living, or a sense of awe, wonder, or fear, which is the root of religion; but rather the question what to do with the feeling for the mystery of living, what to do with awe, wonder or fear (*GSM* 108).

"What to do" with these feelings is taken up in the second and third paths.

The path to God through revelation

With regard to the Bible, Heschel writes, "This generation does not know how to study nor what to study. We have lost the way that

---

8. Heschel, *Man is Not Alone*, 9. Cited hereafter as *MNA*.

leads us to the Bible. We do not learn how to sense the presence of God in the words of the Bible."[9]

With his second path, Heschel intends to show us a way to encounter God through the words of the Bible, as he says, "The presence of God is found in many ways, but above all God is found in the words of the Bible."[10]

Heschel understands that the modern mind, raised in a tradition of rationalism and skepticism, wants proof of the authenticity of revelation. But proof relies on reason, and Heschel points out that reason and science on the one hand, and revelation on the other, work on different levels:

> The Bible and science do not deal with the same problem.... Science deals with relations among things within the universe, but man is endowed with the concern of the spirit, and spirit deals with the relationship between the universe and God. Science seeks the truth about the universe; the spirit seeks the truth that is greater than the universe. Reason's goal is the exploration and verification of objective relations; religion's goal is the exploration and verification of ultimate personal relations (*GSM* 16–19).

Nonetheless, Heschel attempts to use reason to "prove" the truth of revelation. How does he do it? By trying to show that the prophets were authentic. In his examination of the prophets, Heschel says there are only three ways of looking at these Biblical figures. Either "they told the truth, deliberately invented a tale, or were victims of an illusion." He dismisses the second possibility based on the improbability of prophets, "men of highest passion for truth," conspiring over many years to deceive the people of Israel. He discounts the third based on the widespread recognition of the prophets' wisdom: "Their message being ages ahead of human thinking, it would be hard to believe in the normalcy of our minds if we questioned theirs" (*GSM* 223, 227).

---

9. Heschel, *Insecurity of Freedom*, 220. Cited hereafter as *IF*.
10. Granfield, *Theologians at Work*, 77.

Heschel is not attempting to prove the authenticity of the prophets in any traditional sense. He admits that there are no empirical criteria for proving conclusively that the prophets were right or that the Bible is true. Rather, he is trying to show that the authenticity of the prophets can't be conclusively *disproved*. If it can't be disproved, it may be true. In effect, Heschel is demonstrating that reason is not an obstacle to accepting revelation as true, but it is also not—and can never be—the key. Reason is one step. To take that final step, from the possibility of revelation to the certainty of revelation, one must have faith.

> The goal of our "examination" of the prophets was not to furnish the prophets with a letter of recommendation, but rather to point to the difficulty of an outright rejection of their claims. Proofs cannot open the gates of mystery for all men to behold. The only thing we can do is to open the gates of our own soul for God to behold us, to open the gates of our minds and to respond to the words of the prophets (*GSM* 233–34).

Once we "open the gates of our own soul" to belief in the truth of revelation, we can go on to more specific questions: What does revelation mean? Where did revelation come from? To understand Heschel's views on these questions, we first must understand the three major views of revelation in modern Judaism.

The oldest view of revelation was formulated by the rabbis. They believed that the Torah in the broadest sense, including the Mishnah, Talmud, and Haggadah, was revealed by God to Moses. The great medieval Jewish philosophers, including Moses Maimonides (1135–1204) and Moses Nachmanides (1194–1270), accepted this formulation. Today, modern Orthodox Jewish thinkers continue to concur with this view of the Torah.

The first major break with this traditional idea of revelation came from the Reform movement. In order to understand the revolutionary concept of revelation formulated by the Reform movement, let us consider one of its major platforms.

> God reveals himself not only in the majesty, beauty and orderliness of nature, but also in the vision of moral

striving of the human spirit. Revelation is a continuous process, confined to no one group and no one age. Yet the people of Israel, through its prophets and sages, achieved unique insights in the realm of religious truth. The Torah, both written and oral, enshrines Israel's ever-growing consciousness of God and of the moral law.[11]

It is quite apparent that this interpretation of revelation conflicts with the Orthodox position. According to the Reform view, it does not simply flow from God to human beings. Revelation comes about through the insight and discovery of human beings. Human beings, in response to God's inspiration, are the creators of the Bible, yet the statement "God reveals Himself" suggests that the truths discovered by human beings are the truths of God. This would seem to be the implication of the meaning of revelation that is presented by one of the major Reform theologians of the twentieth century, Rabbi Bernard Bamberger.

The adherents of modern liberal religion profess the theory of "progressive revelation." They believe, that is, that the truth of God is made manifest through the continuing search of all men for enlightenment and goodness. All the scientists, poets, philosophers and religious teachers are the channels of God's revelation to mankind.[12]

A third unique view of revelation, in opposition to both the traditional and the Reform views, prevails in the contemporary world. The major spokesman for this position was Martin Buber (1878–1965), whose works have become important for many thinkers today. In what is now a famous passage, Buber presents his position on revelation:

---

11. Plant, *The Growth*, 97.

12. Bamberger, *The Bible*, 89–90. It appears to me that this concept of revelation is closer to the Hindu understanding of revelation than to the traditional Jewish concept. "For the orthodox, the Veda is eternal, and not the product of human minds. Yet it is not like the Bible or the Koran; it is the record of the truth as it was 'discovered' by the great *rishis*, or saints of ancient time rather than a revelation from God." Embree, *Hindu Tradition*, 6.

> My own belief in revelation . . . does not mean that I believe that finished statements about God were handed down from heaven to earth. Rather it means that the human substance is melted by the spiritual fire which visits, and there now breaks from it a word, a statement, which is human in its meaning and form, human conception and human speech, and yet witnesses to Him who stimulated it and to His will.[13]

As Maurice Friedman perceptively says, "Buber rejects the either-or of revelation as objective or subjective in favor of the understanding of revelation as dialogical."[14]

There is certainly an affinity between Heschel's and Buber's approaches to revelation. Both agree that revelation must be viewed as a dialogue between the prophet and God, and contend the prophet "is not a passive recipient" (GSM 259). Heschel says, "prophecy consists of a revelation of God and a co-revelation of man. . . . Thus the Bible is more than the word of God: it is the word of God and man; a record of both revelation and response" (*GSM* 269–70).

But Buber's position that "the laws of the Bible are only the human response to revelation and, therefore, are not binding on future generations,"[15] is very problematic for Heschel, as it is for the entire Jewish tradition. For Buber, "the core of revelation is not the communication of content but the event of God's presence."[16] Heschel's view of revelation as both an event and a content that is binding on all future generations brings him much closer to traditional Judaism than to either the Reform or Buberian view.

To understand the binding content of the Bible, we turn to Heschel's third path, the way to God through the commandments.

---

13. Buber, *Eclipse*, 135.
14. Friedman, *Buber*, 246.
15. Friedman, *Encyclopedia Judaica*, Vol. 4, 1433.
16. Fackenheim, "Buber's Concept," 290.

The path to God through holy deeds

Heschel stresses that "life is a partnership of God and man," and he argues that "this is why human life is holy." It is at this moment that we are able to comprehend fully not only why God entered into a "marriage contract" with Israel but also the importance of mitzvot; the mitzvot are the way that the "partnership," the "marriage contract" between Israel and God is fulfilled.[17]

Heschel's position is that the person who is open to the holy dimension, who is aware of the presence of the ineffable, and for whom revelation becomes a reality will realize that Judaism is not only a religion of love, but is also a religion of yoke: "The first thing a Jew is told is 'You can't let yourself go; get into harness, carry the yoke of the Kingdom of Heaven. . . . The predominant feature of Jewish teaching throughout the ages is a sense of constant obligation.[18] We are obligated to God not only in the way we think, but also in the way we live our everyday life. Heschel repeatedly emphasizes that Judaism is a way of thinking *and* a way of living (*GSM* 197). Although Heschel is perhaps best known for his study of the inner life of the pious man, he understood that the spiritual life of the Jew is determined by his concrete actions. Heschel is true to the Jewish tradition when he states that "man is above all a commanded being, a being of whom demands may be made" (*WM* 107).

> The soul is endowed with a sense of indebtedness, and wonder, awe and fear unlock that sense of indebtedness. Wonder is the state of our being asked. . . . We are driven by an awareness that something is asked of us, that we are asked to wonder, to revere, to think, and to live in a way compatible with the grandeur and mystery of living." (*WM* 109-10).

---

17. Heschel, "Sacred Image," 60. For an excellent discussion of the "marriage contract" metaphor to describe the relationship between God and Israel, see Jakob J. Petuchowski, *Ever Since Sinai*.

18. Heschel, "Religion," 13.

From this quote it is possible to perceive the interrelationship between the different aspects of Heschel's "path to God." The way begins with our response to the world with wonder and awe; this in turn leads to action, to the performance of sacred deeds. Heschel writes, "Sacred deeds are designed to make living compatible with our sense of the ineffable. The mitzvot are forms of expressing in deeds the appreciation of the ineffable" (*GSM* 350).

In his movement from the ineffable to mitzvot, Heschel makes what Maurice Friedman refers to as "the transition from his general philosophy of religion to his specific philosophy of Judaism."[19] Any man or woman can respond to God with wonder; any person open to traditional Western religion can accept the authenticity of revelation; but only the Jew is expected to perform mitzvot. Heschel develops this philosophy in *Man's Quest for God* and in the third part of his major work *God in Search of Man*, which is titled "Response."

What is Heschel's understanding of "Response"? By response Heschel means worship of God (*avodat Ha-Bore*), which encompasses all the commandments (*mitzvot*), including prayer. Heschel believes that the modern Jew who begins to sense the ineffable in the world and in the Bible will respond with acts of worship.

For the modern Jew who still cannot open his or her eyes, however, Heschel presents a most challenging and provocative claim. He contends that the mitzvot, the performance of the commandments, is not merely our response to the demands of God, *they may also serve as a path to God's presence.*

> A Jew is asked to take a leap of action rather than a leap of thought. He is asked to surpass his needs, to do more than he understands in order to understand more than he does. In carrying out the words of the Torah he is ushered into the presence of spiritual meaning. Through the ecstasy of deeds he learns to be certain of the hereness of God. Right living is a way to right thinking (*GSM* 283).

---

19. Friedman, "Liberal Judaism," 24.

Interfaith Activism

Further along, Heschel explains more fully why the Jew is asked to take a "leap of action":

> The mitzvah is a supreme source of religious insight and experience. The way to God is a way of God, and the mitzvah is a way of God, a way where the self-evidence of the Holy is disclosed . . . a mitzvah is where God and man meet.
>
> To meet Him means to come upon an inner certainty of His realness, upon an awareness of His will. Such a meeting, such presence we experience in deeds (*GSM* 312).

Heschel's contention that "the mitzvah is a supreme source of religious insight" helps us understand more fully the interrelationship between the three different aspects of his "path to God." The outline of *God in Search of Man* leads us to believe that the path moves from the ineffable to the reality of revelation and finally to worship. Here, however the direction of the path is reversed. The mitzvot may lead one to sense the ineffable, then to the study of the Torah. If the roads to the Bible and the ineffable are closed, the "leap of action" is an alternate route to discovering God in our lives.

A number of contemporary Jewish thinkers who are receptive to Heschel's thought and have praised his work, including Maurice Friedman, find this "leap of action" problematic. Friedman writes:

> But if we who are not observant Jews do not now feel ourselves commanded by God to perform the law, how can we perform it with integrity even on the strength of Heschel's assurance that we shall know this to be God's will for us through our observance?[20]

Rabbi Dudley Weinberg holds something of the same position when considering the phenomenon of prayer:

> How utterly appropriate is the inscription so frequently inscribed over the ark in our synagogues: *Da lifne mee attah ohmed*—"Know before Whom you stand." Without this recognition prayer can never occur. Introspection

---

20. Ibid., 24.

may occur; we may engage in psychological self-examination; we may study liturgical texts and even find them interesting as sources of stimulating ideas; but prayer cannot occur.[21]

Heschel responds in several ways to these criticisms. Heschel was well aware of the view found in rabbinic and medieval sources that without devotion to God (*kavanah*) the performance of the mitzvot is worthless. He even quotes the extreme view found in the Talmud: "the Rabbis call a person who performs a commandment without the proper intention a transgressor" (*GSM* 408). He is also highly critical of those who would perform mitzvot without any concern for proper intention, "as if all that mattered is how men behaved in physical terms; as if religion were not concerned with the inner life."[22]

But Heschel defends against this possibility by explaining that his "leap of action" may be a key to knowledge of God:

> Judaism insists upon the deed and hopes for the intention. . . . While constantly keeping the goal in mind, we are taught that one must continue to observe the law even when one is not ready to fulfill it "for the sake of God." For the good, even if it is not done for its own sake, will teach us eventually how to act for the sake of God (*GSM* 403–4; *IF* 140–41).

Nonetheless, Heschel would agree with Friedman that the Jew who does not feel commanded by God to perform the mitzvah does not perform it with integrity. But in his important article "Confusion of Good and Evil," Heschel meets the question of integrity itself in a new way. In this article, profoundly influenced by kabbalistic and Hasidic thought, Heschel argues that even the saint cannot perform the commandments with complete integrity. He cites the Jewish mystical view that "in this world neither good nor evil exists in purity, and that there is no good without the admixture of evil nor evil without the admixture of good" (*IF* 134).

---

21. Weinberg, "Prayer," 124.
22. Heschel, *Man's Quest for God*, 53–54. Cited hereafter as *MQG*.

INTERFAITH ACTIVISM

Heschel then raises the question, "If an act to be good must be done exclusively for the sake of God, are we ever able to do the good?" and responds to his question in the following way: although our deeds may never become perfect, will never become entirely free of self-interest, there is great value in their performance and in our struggle to attain greater integrity (*IF* 140).

Further, contemporary Jews are in a uniquely precarious position. The majority lives among Christians in a Christian world and are exposed to the Christian emphasis on love rather than yoke, on faith rather than action. Heschel writes: "Paul waged a passionate battle against the power of law and proclaimed instead the religion of grace. Law, he claimed, cannot conquer sin, nor can righteousness be attained through works of law. A man is justified "by faith without the deeds of law" (*GSM* 293).

Attempting to re-center assimilated Jews' attitudes, he writes, "The first word in God's approach to man is: "The Lord God commanded the man..." (Gen 2:16). It is the commandment we must first listen to (*IF* 174–5).

The danger today is not Jews performing mitzvot without proper intention, but Jews neglecting the mitzvot altogether. Better they perform the mitzvot without intention, says Heschel, than not perform the mitzvot at all.[23]

Thus far we have dealt with only one aspect of worship, the performance of holy deeds. The two other aspects of worship are study of Torah and prayer. Since the rabbinic tradition considers prayer to be a commandment, Heschel deals with prayer in his discussion of the third path. Throughout his works, Heschel repeats the idea that God needs man, and we can interpret this to mean that God needs man's worship. Heschel argues that even

---

23. It is interesting to point out that the Lubavitcher Hasidim are in full agreement with this controversial position of Heschel's. For many years now the Lubavitcher movement has been engaged in a Tefillin campaign, whereby Jewish strangers are approached and asked to put on tefillin. The leaders of this movement are certainly aware that these Jews who are encouraged to put on tefillin and pray will do so without kavanah (devotion to God). Apparently they believe, like Heschel, that the repeated performance of this action may eventually lead to true intention.

in Talmudic times the rabbis debated this issue of whether or not God needs man's worship. A reading of the Midrash reveals many statements supporting Heschel's contention that there were rabbis in Talmudic times who emphasized God's need for human worship. The following Midrash is a good example. "Why were the matriarchs barren? R. Levi said in R. Shila's name and R. Helbo in R. Johanan's name: Because the Holy One, blessed be he, yearns for their prayers and supplications.[24]

For Heschel the great power of worship lies precisely in the fact that God needs man's prayers. Heschel writes:

> Moreover we must not overlook one of the profound principles of Judaism. There is something which is far greater than my desire to pray, namely God's desire that I pray. . . . How insignificant is the outpouring of my soul in the midst of this great universe! Unless it is the will of God that I pray, unless God desires our prayers, how ludicrous is all my praying! (*MQG* 62)

The following statement presents Heschel's central contention about prayer.

> Great is the power of prayer. For to worship is to expand the presence of God in the world. God is transcendent, but our worship makes Him immanent. This is implied in the idea that God is in need of man: His being immanent depends on us (*MQG* 62).

By explaining to us the idea of a God of pathos and by offering us a three-fold path to encounter God, Abraham Joshua Heschel has given us an innovative way to understand religion that is at the same time grounded in Jewish tradition. In his review of *Man Is Not Alone*, the book which is devoted primarily to the first path, Maurice Friedman claims, "Actually, *Man Is Not Alone* has as much power to speak to the uncommitted as any book that American Jewish thought has produced."[25] Through the first path Heschel shows us how to see the spiritual dimension of the world.

---

24. Rabbah, *Genesis, Vol. 1*, 381.
25. Friedman, "Heschel," 2.

Interfaith Activism

The second path shows a way to access the ancient scriptures. In the third path, a specifically Jewish path, he shows us how to live a life of mitzvot that could help us find God.

For Heschel, the contemplation of the role of human beings and their relationship to God was never simply a form of intellectual gamesmanship. It is important; it is vital; there are drastic stakes. As Heschel says:

> Mankind will not die for lack of information. It will perish for lack of appreciation. Unless there is appreciation there is no mankind. The great marvel of being alive is the ability to discover the mystery and wonder of everything. . . . Unless we learn how to revere, we will not know how to exist as human beings (*MNA* 37).

> Heschel's path to God brings out the spiritual dimension of Judaism, a Judaism that can no longer be dismissed as a dry religion. For Heschel authentic Judaism is essentially "a way of developing sensitivity to God and attachment to His presence" (*GSM* 26).

Soon after Heschel's major books began to appear in the 1950s, Christian thinkers did not fail to see the profound nature of his work. Reinhold Niebuhr, the great Protestant theologian of the twentieth century, in his review of *Man Is Not Alone*, wrote: "This volume is so impressive because it is the work of a poet and mystic who has mastered the philosophical and scientific disciplines and who with consummate skill reveals the dimension of reality apprehended by religious faith."[26] By the time of his death, Heschel had emerged as an important authentic Jewish voice among Jews and members of other religious traditions. The prominent Hindu scholar K. Sivaraman wrote, "Heschel is one of my favorite thinkers of religion of this century."[27] The Christian scholar W. D. Davies stated, "I speak for Christians and other non-Jews. To encounter

---

26. Niebuhr, "Masterly Analysis."
27. K. Sivaraman, letter to Harold Kasimow, Feb. 3, 1986.

him [Heschel] was to 'feel' the force and spirit of Judaism, the depth and grandeur of it."[28]

I believe that today, Heschel's works are more widely read than ever before and that his path to God still has the power to move the hearts and minds of contemporary human beings.

---

28. Davies, "Conscience," 214.

2

Heschel's View of Religious Diversity

A FEW WEEKS BEFORE he died in 1972, my teacher, Abraham Joshua Heschel, left the following message for young people: "And above all, remember that the meaning of life is to build a life as if it were a work of art. You're not a machine. And you are young. Start working on this great work of art called your own existence."[1] If what Heschel says is true, if one's existence is a work of art, then Heschel's was a masterpiece. He was one of the most significant, religious thinkers of the last century, one who at the same time was deeply engaged in the social issues of his day. He was both a committed, passionate Jew and an "apostle to the gentiles" who was revered by many Christians and considered a *tzaddik*, a saint, by Jews. He publicly opposed the Vietnam War, he was active in the civil rights movement, and he worked vigorously to help Jews suffering in the Soviet Union. What stood out about Heschel was his ability to speak as a Jew, but a Jew who could communicate beyond the boundaries of his own religious tradition. My good friend, the Catholic theologian John Merkle, said it best: "In his own life and works, Abraham Joshua Heschel revealed the supreme importance of God as well as what it is like to live with faith in God."[2]

1. Stern, "Interview," 412.
2. Merkle, *Genesis*, 26.

Heschel's View of Religious Diversity

In his essay "Heschel's Impact on Catholic-Jewish Relations," Dr. Eugene Fisher, Executive Secretary of the Secretariat for Catholic-Jewish Relations of the National Conference of Catholic Bishops, writes:

> Heschel's work and life, of course, were particularly profound in their influence on American Catholics of my generation. His thought spiritually enriched us as his courageous deeds—whether marching for civil rights or against the Vietnam War—prophetically challenged us. To many of us in the Catholic community active in the 1960s, Abraham Joshua Heschel, along with Thomas Merton and Dorothy Day, were perceived as no less than contemporary prophets, searing our souls, and enflaming our vision with God's hope for a better humanity. Through him we learned to understand, to feel, what it means to say that the Bible is the living word of God.[3]

Furthermore, Heschel played a major role in shaping the church's view of Judaism. He was the most important Jewish voice during the meeting of the Second Vatican Council (1962–1965). Heschel spent a great deal of time with Augustine Cardinal Bea, SJ, who, at that time, headed the Secretariat for Promoting Christian Unity and was responsible for drafting the church's revolutionary renunciation of anti-Semitism in *Nostra Aetate*. Heschel even convinced Pope Paul VI to remove an offensive paragraph that (against Cardinal Bea's wishes) called for Jews to convert to Christianity. After this document came out, Heschel said that what was of greatest significance for him was "the omission of any reference to conversion of the Jews."[4]

Heschel was beloved by Christians, especially by Catholic thinkers, for his profound religious thought and the inspiring way he lived. But what did Heschel think of Christianity, as well as other traditions? Did he feel that Judaism was the only true religion? Did he feel that all religions are equally valid? How did this committed Jewish thinker grapple with the question of religious difference?

---

3. Fisher, "Heschel's Impact," 111.
4. Heschel, *Vatican II*, 373.

Interfaith Activism

Many Christian theologians consider religious diversity to be one of the most important issues of our time. It is now nearly fifty years since the distinguished Christian theologian and historian of religion Wilfred Cantwell Smith spoke these words concerning religious diversity: "This is really as big an issue, almost, as the question of how one accounts theologically for evil—but Christian theologians have been much more conscious of the fact of evil than that of religious pluralism."[5] Since that time, numerous Christian theologians have struggled to arrive at a Christian theology of religions that would be consistent with the new awareness of religious diversity. A number of prominent Christian theologians who have contemplated the issue of religious diversity speak of three major models: exclusivist, inclusivist, and pluralist.[6] Traditionally, Christians, like believers of many other faiths concerning their religion, have seen Christianity as the only true path to salvation and all other paths as false. This is the exclusivist view.

The inclusivist response is more positive about other religions. According to this approach, the grace of Christ is present in other traditions; therefore, members of other religions may attain salvation. The eminent Jesuit theologian Karl Rahner (1904–1984) developed the inclusivist view, which had advocates in the early church, in great detail. Rahner, who was very influential in the Second Vatican Council, claimed the Christian tradition is "the absolute religion, intended for all men, which can't recognize any other religion beside itself as of equal right."[7] However, since God desires to save all human beings, "there are supernatural, grace-filled elements in non-Christian religions."[8] Pope John Paul II, the world's most famous inclusivist, stated, "Respect and esteem for the other and for what he has in the depths of his heart is essential to dialogue."[9]

---

5. Smith, *The Faith*, 121.

6. Alan Race, editor of the journal *Interreligious Insight*, develops these models in great detail. See his book *Christians and Religious Pluralism*.

7. Rahner, "Christianity," 56.

8. Ibid., 61.

9. John Paul II, "To Representatives," 218.

Heschel's View of Religious Diversity

Pluralism takes an even more expansive view of other religions. Paul Knitter, a prominent Catholic theologian, has presented the pluralist perspective in a most perceptive and persuasive way:

> Other religions may be just as effective and successful in bringing their followers to truth, and peace, and wellbeing with God as Christianity has been for Christians. ... Only if Christians are truly open to the possibility ... that there are many true, saving religions and that Christianity is one among the ways in which God has touched and transformed our world—only then can authentic dialogue take place.[10]

John Hick, the best-known exponent of the pluralist position, explains that for the pluralist it is fundamental that one not elevate one's own religion to a status that is regarded "as uniquely superior to all the others."[11] That means, among other things, that when we come to metaphysical claims about God we cannot consider a personal vision of God as superior to an impersonal one. We cannot say that mysticism of personality is superior to mysticism of infinity or that theistic mysticism is superior to monistic mysticism. With regard to sacred texts, the religious pluralists will say that he or she is committed to following the Torah or the Vedas or the Qu'ran or the New Testament not because that sacred text is superior to other sacred texts but because it is the sacred text of his or her religious tradition.

Generally, Jewish thinkers have not given the same level of attention to religious diversity as Christian theologians. Heschel remains the most significant Jewish thinker to address this critical issue. In his essay "No Religion Is an Island," he presents a radical view of the world's religions. Heschel argues that no religion has a monopoly on truth or holiness and says, "In this aeon diversity of religions is the will of God."[12] This statement is certainly open to different interpretations. I believe that it means that Heschel accepted the validity of other religious traditions. By saying that

---

10. Knitter, *One Earth*, 30.
11. Hick, "Next Step," 6.
12. Heschel, "No Religion," 14.

Interfaith Activism

religions are the will of God, I believe he means there is also a divine element in these traditions. Heschel cites a Talmudic source that clearly supports this interpretation. "It is a well-established tradition in Jewish literature that the Lord sent prophets to the nations, and even addressed Himself directly to them."[13] According to Heschel, "The Jews do not maintain that the way of the Torah is the only way of serving God."[14]

Long before Heschel, the Jewish tradition taught that the righteous of all nations have a share in the world to come. Heschel cites a rabbinic source that I consider important for our time: "I call heaven and earth to witness that the Holy Spirit rests upon each person, Jew or Gentile, man or woman, master or slave, in consonance with his deeds."[15] For Heschel, it is less important what religious path people follow than that they show compassion for their fellow human beings. For Heschel, "Religion is a means, not an end."[16] He says, "The prophets convey to us the certainty that human life is sacred, that the most important thing a person can do is to have compassion for his fellow man."[17] The end of religion is to ennoble, to refine, to transform us so that we really have concern for others—which makes us truly human. This teaching is in keeping with his idea that God's outstanding characteristic is "divine pathos." In Heschel's mind, the ultimate goal of human life is to care about humanity as much as God does. This vision enables him to see the saintliness among many of the Christians whom he encountered.

In view of Heschel's stress that "diversity of religions is the will of God" and that "the Jews do not maintain that the way of the Torah is the only way of serving God," should we then see him as a Jewish pluralist? While Heschel sees all religions as valid, he does not see them as fundamentally equal. A study of Heschel's works reveals that he was quite familiar with some of the primary

13. Heschel, *The Prophets*, 226.
14. Heschel, "No Religion," 19.
15. Ibid., 18.
16. Granfield, *Theologians*, 78.
17. Heschel, "Eternal Light," 8.

sources of Christianity and Islam as well as those of Hinduism and Buddhism. In his interpretation of these sources, he stresses the unique aspects of each religion, its distinctiveness and particularity. He is critical of certain aspects of Asian thought as well as of certain doctrines of Judaism and Christianity. His critique of other religions suggests that Heschel differs from pluralists like Hick. While he does not hold that Judaism is the only true religion and agrees with Knitter and Hick that all religious traditions produce saints, he does not see all traditions as equal. They are all valid, but they are not *equally* valid.

For Heschel, the most fundamental concept of biblical thought is that God is in search of human beings, that God is a God of pathos who needs human beings and is affected by their actions. Heschel's entire theological structure rests on the assumption that there is a personal God, a God who commands and makes demands on human beings, who is concerned and involved with human beings. Heschel has great difficulty with any system of thought that does not involve a personal concept of God.

In *God in Search of Man*, his most famous work, Heschel says the Hebrew Bible is superior to other sacred texts. Heschel states: "The Bible is mankind's greatest privilege. It is so . . . categorical in its demands and full of compassion in its understanding of the human situation. No other book so loves and respects the life of man" (*GSM* 239). Heschel then raises the questions, "Why does the Bible surpass everything created by man? Why is there no work worthy of comparison with it? Why is there no substitute for the Bible, no parallel to the history it has engendered? Why must all who seek the living God turn to its pages?" (*GSM 240*) Heschel responds to his own questions thus: "Set the Bible beside any of the truly great books produced by the genius of man, and see how they are diminished in stature. . . . Other books you can estimate, you can measure, compare; the Bible you can only extol. Its insights surpass our standards. There is nothing greater" (*GSM* 240). He concludes by saying "just as it is impossible to conceive of God without the world, so it is impossible to conceive of His concern without the Bible. . . . If God is alive, then the Bible is His voice. No other work is as worthy of being considered a manifestation of His will" (*GSM* 245).

Heschel's elevation of the Hebrew Bible seems to suggest that he has an inclusivist rather than a pluralist perspective. Christian inclusivists like John Paul II would agree with Heschel when he states that the aim of dialogue is to overcome "hardness of heart" and to cultivate "a sense of wonder and mystery in unlocking doors to holiness in time" (*GSM* 245). But Heschel differs radically from Christian inclusivists in his opposition to conversion and the creation of a monolithic religious society. And of course his view of the Hebrew Bible being the greatest religious book is not analogous to the Pope's view that sees Jesus as the only source of God's salvation and therefore sees interreligious dialogue as part of the church's evangelizing mission.

Heschel's view of other faiths, including the aim of dialogue and his opposition to evangelism, is remarkably similar to the view of Tenzin Gyatso, the fourteenth Dalai Lama, one of the most loved and respected religious leaders in the world today, who is seen by Buddhists as a living incarnation of a Buddha. For the Dalai Lama, as for Heschel, the fact that there are different religions is something beautiful that should be celebrated. But religions are not equally valid.

The Dalai Lama believes that from a Buddhist perspective one does not attain liberation while still attached to the idea of a permanent self. There is no enduring person, a permanent self, or an immortal soul, as Jews and Christians claim. For the Dalai Lama, as for many Mahayana Buddhists, the Buddha had different teachings for different people. From this perspective, other great religious teachers and founders of religions may be seen as *bodhisattvas* who use skillful means to bring to the world a preliminary teaching such as the concept of a personal savior god. To the question put to him at "the Bodhgaya interviews"—"But is it only the Buddha who can be the ultimate source of refuge?"—the Dalai Lama responded:

> Liberation in which "a mind that understands the sphere of reality annihilates all defilements in the sphere of

reality" is a state that only Buddhists can accomplish. This kind of *moksa* or nirvana is only explained in the Buddhist scriptures, and is achieved only through Buddhist practice. According to certain religions, however, salvation is a place, a beautiful paradise, like a peaceful valley. To attain such a state as this, to achieve such a state of *moksa*, does not require the practice of emptiness, the understanding of reality.[18]

This statement by the Dalai Lama is not consistent with John Hicks' view of other faiths. It seems to me that both the Dalai Lama and Heschel viewed their own traditions as somehow better. Both are deeply committed to their own paths, yet they are opposed to proselytism and make no claim that they have exclusive possession of ultimate truth. I repeat Heschel's statements: "Holiness is not the monopoly of any religion or tradition" and that "the Jews do not maintain that the way of the Torah is the only way of God."

In one of his best-known books, the Dalai Lama writes in a similar vein when he states:

> In my own case, I am convinced that Buddhism provides me with the most effective framework within which to situate my efforts to develop spiritually through cultivating love and compassion. At the same time, I must acknowledge that while Buddhism represents the best path for me—that is, it suits my character, my temperament, my inclinations, and my cultural background—the same will be true of Christianity for Christians. For them, Christianity is the best way. On the basis of my conviction, I cannot, therefore, say that Buddhism is best for everyone.[19]

In this book the core message of the Dalai Lama is the necessity of love and compassion. This is precisely the message of Heschel, who claimed, "The greatest heresy is despair of men's power for goodness, men's power for love" (*IF* 98). In the Jewish tradition we are commanded to love all human beings because

---

18. Dalai Lama, *Bodhgaya Interviews*, 23.
19. Dalai Lama, *Ethics*, 225–26.

all are created in the image of God. For Heschel, as for the great sage Rabbi Akiva, the supreme principle of the Torah is "love thy neighbor as thyself."

Heschel was very much in love with the Jewish tradition. He loved the Jewish people. But his greatness lies in his ability to extend this love to everyone and to see the humanity and touch of divinity in all religious traditions. His love and compassion have brought great healing and great hope to all who have encountered him through the example of his life and the eloquence of his written word.

In his unique view of religious diversity, Heschel is neither pluralist nor inclusivist. I now see him as a Jewish interreligious artist who transcends the categories created by Christian scholars. Heschel was a committed Jew, who, on the one hand, was able to affirm and live out the consequences of the fact that no religion has a monopoly on truth or holiness, and, on the other hand, that the Hebrew Bible is "the only book in the whole world that can never be replaced"(*GSM* 240).

3

Spiritual Masters in the Jewish Tradition

> And ye shall be unto Me a kingdom of priests, and a holy nation. (Exod 19:6)
>
> Ye shall be holy; for I the Lord Your God am holy. (Lev 19:2)

WHEN I RECENTLY TOLD a rabbi that I was writing an essay on Jewish saints, he was somewhat puzzled. I am not surprised. When Jews think about saints, they usually think of Christianity. They think of the Catholic process of beatification and canonization by which the church declares a person to be a saint. In Judaism there is no official religious body that can recognize someone as a saint. But there are saints in the Jewish tradition. When a person lives a holy, pious life, the Jewish community may come to recognize that human being as a saint. In the Jewish tradition a saint, or a spiritual master, may be called a *talmid hakham* (disciple of the wise), *tzaddik* (a righteous person), or hasid (pious person). There are also other terms for the spiritually elite in the Jewish tradition, such as *ga'on* (genius) and *gadol hador* (the Torah leader of the generation).

But how does Judaism define a saint? I would define a saint as a person who views *Imitatio Dei* as the ultimate purpose of life,[1] and who is totally committed to the following two commandments from the Torah: "You must love the Lord your God with all your heart and with all your soul and with all your might" (Deut 6:4) and "Love your neighbor as yourself" (Lev 19:17).[2] The test of a holy life is the willingness to give up one's life for the sake of the commandments. Saints are always ready to die for God.

Because the Jewish tradition places such a strong emphasis on study, on the mind, the Jewish saint will most likely come from the ranks of the *talmid hakhamim*, a sage who has mastered the Torah in an astonishing way and attained great stature in the community.[3] Classical Judaism sees such a person as the ideal because the Torah is believed to be the word of God and study of the Torah is seen as "holiness in words." Study, it is said, not only leads to paradise; it itself is paradise. By studying the Torah we can discern the will of God and fulfill all the *mitzvot* (commandments).[4] The

---

1. Schechter (1847–1915) in his classic book, *Aspects of Rabbinic Theology* presents a very helpful analysis of holiness in rabbinic literature. He discerns a distinction between holiness and saintliness which is not always made clear by the rabbis. In his discussion of holiness and saintliness, he states that "the former moves more within the limits of the Law, though occasionally exceeding it, while the latter, aspiring to a superior kind of holiness, not only supplements the Law, but also proves a certain corrective to it" (201). His later comment on rabbinic Judaism is very helpful in showing the affinity between Judaism and Christianity: "Impure thinking was, in the rabbinic view, the antecedent to impure doing, and the ideal saint was as pure of heart as of hand, acting no impurity and thinking none" (210–11).

2. Jesus was reflecting Jewish thinking when he cited these two commandments as the most important verses of the Torah. See Mark 12:28-34. In this essay, scriptural passages from the Hebrew Bible are from the 1955 and 1962 translations of *The Holy Scriptures* by the Jewish Publication Society of America.

3. *Pirke Avot*, the best-known rabbinic text, teaches that "the ignoramus will not be saintly" (Avot 2:5). *Pirke Avot* is the only part of the Talmud that was incorporated into the Jewish prayer book. The rabbis stated: "Whoever aspires to saintliness, let him fulfill the teaching of avot" (Baba Kamma, 30a).

4. Jewish mystics go even further. For them, the words of the Torah are a rendezvous point where humans meet God, who is "in the letters of the Torah." So, study is a way toward *devekut*, and not only a way of discerning God's will.

person who submits to God's will and fulfills both the ritual *mitzvot* and the ethical *mitzvot* becomes holy.

The Jewish tradition sees Rabbi Elijah ben Solomon of Vilna (1720-1797), who is known as the Vilna Gaon and who studied Torah eighteen hours a day, as the ideal spiritual master in the Jewish tradition. He was known as *ha-Ga'on he-Hasid*.[5]

However, some Jews who are not great scholars may also be considered saints. They may be recognized as saints because of their intense love of God or their humility or because they may be blessed with divine inspiration which gives them special power to influence God. The greatest challenge to the classical conception of a Jewish saint was the Baal Shem Tov (1700-1760), the founder of the Hasidic movement, who did not come from the ranks of the *talmid hakhamim* and was not known for his extraordinary knowledge of the Torah. The Baal Shem Tov gave greater emphasis to the heart than to the mind. He himself was a teacher of small children and a laborer who spent a great deal of time meditating in the forest rather than in the study hall. For the Baal Shem Tov, prayer with concentration, with joy, with ecstasy may be a better way to cleave to God than study of the Torah.

The Baal Shem Tov was viewed by his followers as the ideal saint, the ideal master, the great *tzaddik*. His followers began to emphasize the doctrine of the *tzaddik*, whom they saw as an intermediary between themselves and God. According to the doctrine of the *tzaddik*, if we want to become attached to God we must attach ourselves to the *tzaddik*, whose thoughts are entirely God-centered. According to Louis Jacobs, the Hasidic master Elimelech of Lizensk (1717-1787) claimed that the tzaddik "brings man near to God and he brings down God's grace from heaven to earth."[6]

---

5. In his chapter "The Gaon, Rabbi Elijah Wilna," written in 1928, Louis Ginzberg writes: "The earliest documents in which the Gaon is mentioned, one dating from the time he was thirty, the other from a time when he was thirty-five, call him Rabbi Elijah the Saint, and to this day, his synagogue in Wilna is known as the synagogue of the saint." *Students*, 141.

6. Jacobs, "The Doctrine," 3. Jacobs claims that according to Elimelech of Lizensk "the Zaddik has power over life and death." This power is given by God to the *tzaddik* because "God so desires the prayers of the righteous."

Interfaith Activism

We should not be surprised, therefore, that the Gaon of Vilna banned the Hasidic movement.

Moses Maimonides (1135–1204), the great Jewish philosopher, of whom it is said "From Moses to Moses there was none like Moses," distinguishes between two types of ideal people: the *hakham*, that is, the sage, and the *hasid*, that is, the saint. Rabbi Jonathan Sacks claims that Maimonides favors the sage over the saint because "the sage is concerned with the perfection of society. The saint is concerned with the perfection of self."[7] This is a useful distinction, but it does not always work so neatly in reality. The greatest Jewish sage, the Vilna Gaon, is also seen as a great saint. The sage from Vilna devoted so much time to the study of the Torah that it left him very little time to become involved in the affairs of his community. He never accepted a rabbinic position.

> The Gaon's way of life, as portrayed by his sons and his students, was characterized by the maximum channeling of the powers of body and soul to one exclusive goal: the study of the Torah. In practice, the Gaon understood absolute devotion to Torah study as one side of the coin; the other side was the value of asceticism and withdrawal from society as a guiding principle and way of life. . . . [T]he Gaon saw the main significance of asceticism in its channeling of the majority of an individual's physical and spiritual resources toward the purpose of Torah study. He therefore particularly stressed the value of separation from the society of other people, as social contact brings

---

"Doctrine," 6. To this day, many Hasidim visit the graves of their Hasidic masters because they believe that their masters still retain their miracle-making powers and may intervene on their behalf. In a recent pioneering work entitled *Workers of Wonders*, Byron Sherwin argues that the most influential Jewish leaders throughout history were also miracle workers. The veneration of saints who are believed to be miracle workers was an especially widely practiced phenomenon among North African Jews, who continue this practice today in Israel. (See Weingrod, *The Saint of Beersheba*, and Sherwin, *Workers of Wonders*.) For a more in-depth discussion of the idea of drawing down divine grace, see Sherwin, *Kabbalah*, especially chapter 7. I am deeply grateful to Byron Sherwin for his careful reading of this essay and for his helpful comments.

7. Sacks, *To Heal*, 245; emphasis in the original.

in its wake the loss of time from Torah study, while isolation from society assists in constancy of study.[8]

In his last book, *A Passion for Truth*, Abraham Joshua Heschel points out the affinity that the major Hasidic leader Rabbi Mendel of Kotzk, known as the Kotzker, had for the Gaon of Vilna by citing the following passage about the Gaon:

> The Gaon would not receive people in order to save all his time for his studies. When his sister came to see him after an absence of twelve years, he said to his attendant, "Tell her we'll see each other in the next world. I have no time for such meetings here."[9]

Heschel claims that the Kotzker had a somewhat similar view: "Both lived in solitude, cut off from the world."[10] In his excellent article "Ascetical Aspects of Ancient Judaism," Steven D. Fraade, professor at Yale University, states: "If the central religious obligation is that of the study of Torah (and attachment to God through it), then worldly preoccupations such as family are bound to be distracting for reasons of time, energy, and purity."[11] Here we can see the strong ascetic strain in the Jewish tradition, which we will find in Moses Hayyim Luzzatto's path to holiness.

In contrast, the Baal Shem Tov, who revealed himself as a spiritual master when he was thirty-six years old, did not believe that to live a spiritual life it is necessary to divorce oneself from this world. He stressed a passage from the prophet Isaiah that "the whole world is full of His presence" (Isa 6:1). Even more central to his teaching is his interpretation of the phrase from Proverbs "In all your ways know God" (Prov 3:6). For the Baal Shem Tov, people have different paths to God. Study may not be the path for everyone; each person needs to find the right path for himself. The Baal Shem Tov felt that the highest peak of spiritual living is attained through immersion in everyday life. Heschel's statement on

---

8. Etkes, *Salanter*, 18.
9. Heschel, *Passion*, 82.
10. Ibid., 82.
11. Fraade, "Ascetical Aspects," 274–75.

the Baal Shem Tov helps us see the contrast between the Baal Shem Tov and the Gaon of Vilna:

> Before the Baal Shem's time, pious Jews felt that to be close to God, the body must be chastised, one must fast and scourge oneself. Bodily enjoyment was considered despicable; sexual pleasures filled them with revulsion. But the Baal Shem and his followers held that all delights come from Eden. "A longing for things material is an instrument by which one may approach the love of God; even through coarse desires one may come to love the Creator." Lust, desire, evil inclination, all should be elevated, not uprooted.[12]

"For the Baal Shem Tov," says Heschel, "saintliness and worldliness are not mutually exclusive."[13]

For the Mithnagdim, the traditional Jews who opposed the Hasidim, Hasidic beliefs seem to blur the distinction between the sacred and profane. Especially troubling to them and their leader, the Gaon of Vilna, was the Hasidic sanctification of food and drink. The Gaon of Vilna discouraged excessive eating even on the Sabbath. One of his students recounts the following conversation:

> When I spoke of this matter before my teacher, the Gaon, of blessed memory, he told me that he had a general principle that even though it is a mitzvah to eat and drink on the Sabbath, it is also a mitzvah to study Torah on the Sabbath. It is then much better to increase one's study than to increase one's eating and drinking. For increasing study will help develop study habits, and study is a mitzvah at all other times as well. On the other hand, eating on the Sabbath will lead to a greater appetite on weekdays as well.[14]

It may seem that the Mithnagdic and the Hassidic conceptions of the saint cannot be reconciled. But as I will demonstrate

---

12. Heschel, *Passion*, 25.
13. Ibid., 24.
14. Nadler, *Faith*, 86.

in the third section, there is a modern-day saint who combines the virtues of both models of the saint.

The path to holiness in Jewish thought

We have some sense of what a Jewish saint is. But how does one become a saint? The best description of a path to holiness in the classical Jewish tradition comes from the great Jewish mystic and ethical writer from Italy, Moses Hayyim Luzzatto (1707–1746), and his *Mesillat Yesharim* (The Path of the Upright). Perhaps the most influential Jewish book on ethics, *Mesillat Yesharim* presents a systematic, step-by-step eight-fold path on how to attain holiness: "Holiness is of a twofold nature; it begins as a quality of the service rendered to God, but it ends as a reward for such service. It is at first a type of spiritual effort, and then a kind of spiritual gift. A man must first strive to be holy, and then he is endowed with holiness."[15]

Luzzatto's work is actually an investigation into a single teaching from the second century Rabbi Phinehas ben Yair, who stated: "The knowledge of Torah leads to watchfulness, watchfulness to zeal, zeal to cleanness, cleanness to abstinence, abstinence to purity, purity to saintliness, saintliness to humility, humility to fear of sin, and fear of sin to holiness" (*MY* 18). Luzzatto transformed his hierarchy of qualities into a detailed guide to how man could perfect himself.

Luzzatto based his arguments on the belief that human beings, because they are imbued with a divine soul, cannot be satisfied with anything that can be found in this world. Rather, human beings were created to enjoy the world to come. Luzzatto writes: "Likewise, if thou were to offer the soul all the pleasures of the

---

15. Luzzatto, *Mesillat Yesharim*, 442. I find it somewhat paradoxical that Kaplan (1881–1983), the founder of the Reconstructionist Movement in Judaism, whose reinterpretation of the Jewish tradition rejects the concept of a supernatural God, devoted so much time to translating a text written by one of the greatest mystics that Judaism has produced. In the introduction Kaplan explains why he did so: "*Mesillat Yesharim* will ever serve as a true mirror reflecting the inwardness and spirituality which Judaism demanded of those who lived in conformity with its laws" (xxxvi). Hereafter cited as *MY*.

world, she would remain indifferent to them, because she belongs to a higher order of existence" (*MY* 32). Therefore, this world should be viewed only as a path to fulfillment in the world to come.

Luzzatto says, "All of man's strivings should be directed toward the Creator, blessed be He. A man should have no other purpose in whatever he does, be it great or small, than to draw nigh to God and to break down all separating walls, that is, all things of a material nature, between himself and his Master, so that he may be drawn to God as iron to a magnet" (*MY* 36).

Watchfulness

Following Rabbi Phinehas ben Yair's model, the first step to holiness begins with watchfulness. By watchfulness, Luzzatto means great care to avoid the evil inclination inside oneself. Only by studying the Torah and taking time to consider its ethical lessons can one avoid the evil inclination: "In fine, a man should at all times consider carefully what course to pursue so as to conform with the laws of the Torah. He should also set aside stated periods when he may contemplate in solitude" (*MY* 56). But watchfulness is endangered by three factors: "The first is preoccupation with worldly affairs; the second is frivolity and levity; the third is the society of evil companions" (*MY* 80).

All three factors that endanger watchfulness might compromise one's intent to live by the code of the Torah. Of these three, Luzzatto is most concerned about the danger of involvement in worldly affairs. He feels that this is the most common enemy and also the one factor that is easiest to overcome. At the same time, Luzzatto is opposed to severe asceticism. He realized that a human being must devote a certain amount of time to making a livelihood. But he was certain that devoting one's life to materialism would not deliver lasting bliss or salvation.

Zeal

The next step is zeal. Luzzatto explains that watchfulness pertains to the negative commandments while zeal pertains to the positive ones. He who is watchful merely avoids sin; he who is zealous also does good. Zeal means a commitment to do the *mitzvot* whenever possible. To acquire this commitment is no simple task; it requires great strength. Luzzatto writes:

> It should be borne in mind that it is the nature of man to be inert, and that the earthiness of the physical element in him acts as a weight upon him. Man, therefore, seeks to avoid all toil and effort. Accordingly, a man who desires the privilege of worshiping the Creator, blessed be He, must be able to prevail over his own nature, and act with strength and energy" (*MY* 98).

Cleanness

Luzzatto proceeds to the higher stage of cleanness. He tells us that "The quality of cleanness consists in being free from the evil traits as well as from sin" (*MY* 134). Cleanness of soul is higher than watchfulness and zeal because the person who acquires the stages of watchfulness and zeal only succeeds in keeping his evil inclination in check, but he does not eradicate it. The person who has attained the higher stage of cleanness is beyond the evil inclination—beyond lust, beyond temptation. As a person becomes clean, the fire of lust will die out in his heart and its cessation will bring about a longing for the divine: "The true way to acquire the trait of spiritual cleanness is to read assiduously the words of our Sages, both their legal enactments and their ethical exhortations" (*MY* 234). According to Luzzatto, most people are only capable of reaching the stage of cleanness. Only a few can become saints.

Abstinence

With the next step we begin to approach the stages that lead to sainthood. The stage of abstinence marks the way to saintliness. The great enemy of abstinence is the craving and attachment to the pleasures of the world. The senses are indeed powerful antagonists to the greatest of men and women. The eyes of human beings are captivated by things that are outwardly beautiful and charming. It was these perceptions that "lead to man's original sin, as scripture testifies" (*MY* 262).[16] The way to attain abstinence is by realizing the true nature of pleasures. Luzzatto finds pleasures to be useless, worthless, and transient. Once a human being has attained abstinence he will no longer be allured by physical pleasures, "for he will know that he may enjoy in this world only those things without which he can't live" (*MY* 266).[17]

Purity

Purity follows abstinence. The essence of purity is the perfecting of one's heart and one's thought. Above all, to be pure is to attain

---

16. The English translation of *Mesillat Yesharim* by Shiraga Silverstein translates this Hebrew passage as "first sin" rather than "original sin," which I believe is more in accord with Luzzatto's meaning and the Jewish tradition, which rejects the idea of original sin. (Silverstein, *MY,* 197)

17. With the focus on abstinence, Luzzatto comes dangerously close to creating a monastic movement within Judaism. Following this idea to its logical conclusion one should not marry. Any man who reached this stage would be faced with a real conflict, since he must fulfill the commandment to "be fruitful and multiply." Luzzatto himself was married and had children, for he could not go against the Torah.

It may be asked whether Luzzatto's emphasis on other-worldliness is consistent with what may be called normative Judaism. Dr. Guttmann's statement concerning the very influential medieval Jewish ethical writer Bahya ibn Pakuda helps us understand this point: "Bahya goes far beyond the clues provided by the Talmud; for though the Talmud places man's ultimate aim in the world to come, it does not view the moral and religious task of his life exclusively from the viewpoint of the hereafter." Guttmann, *Philosophies of Judaism,* 123. Seeing the world from the point of view of the world to come is precisely what Luzzatto does throughout his book.

perfect worship: "It can be called perfect only when it is pure and is rendered for no reason except that of serving God" (*MY* 276). Before one reaches this stage one must realize that human glory is vanity, and one must view ambition as merely striving after the wind. Purity is zeal stripped of ego. It is higher than cleanness because cleanness involves only eradicating the evil inclination, while purity involves the actual performance of *mitzvot*. By meditating for many hours one prepares oneself for the performance of a mitzvah and in so doing becomes one with it. Only at this point "will he perform his religious duties with no thought of the praise he might win; his mind will then be directed wholly toward his Master. He alone is our glory, our good, and our perfection" (*MY* 284).

Saintliness

Purity leads to saintliness, which is different in Luzzatto's view from holiness. Man alone can achieve saintliness; holiness requires the intervention of God. Luzzatto compares the saint to a lover who is always ready to do more than what is required. As a lover of God the aim is always to give happiness to one's Creator. Luzzatto devotes four chapters to saintliness, placing great stress on wisdom and the centrality of the study of the Torah. He states: "Saintliness should be reared upon great wisdom and upon the adjustment of conduct to the aims worthy of the truly wise. Only the wise can truly grasp the nature of saintliness; as our Sages said, 'The ignorant man cannot be saintly'" (*MY* 290). The need to attain wisdom by studying Torah day and night may be a major reason why Luzzatto, who clearly favors the world to come over this world, is opposed to prolonged fasting and other ascetic practices. Luzzatto was surely familiar with the rabbinic view that "a Torah scholar may not fast because he is detracting from the work of heaven."[18]

---

18. Diamond, *Holy Men*, 117.

Humility

Also essential for the saint is the practice of loving kindness, which forbids the infliction of pain upon any living creature. The saint's heart must be full of compassion and benevolence. We are faced here with a Jewish version of *ahimsa*, the Hindu belief of nonviolence. Withdrawing to solitude and concentrating upon the truth of the perfect and exalted nature of God will lead the saint to a state in which he ceases to regard himself with self-esteem. At the point at which the saint does not think of himself at all, since his whole being is concerned with the glory of God, he has reached the stage of humility—the all-consuming submission of one to God's will. Constant humility can only be achieved through reflection and training. This means habituating oneself in humbleness until humility is an implicit part of being.

Fear of Sin

The stage of humility is followed by the stage of the fear of sin. By the fear of sin Luzzatto does not mean only the fear of punishment but also a sense of awe for the glory of God. We can see how this sense of awe would be an inevitable result of submitting one's entire self to the will of God. Since Luzzatto believed that the fate of the world depended on our conduct, fearing sin was equivalent to fearing the destruction of the world.

Holiness

While great commitment can allow man to ascend through the first seven stages, the final stage of Luzzatto's path, holiness, is beyond the effort of human beings alone. He writes:

> But since it is impossible for a man to attain this status through his own efforts—for he is, after all, only a physical being, mere flesh and blood—holiness has to be finally

granted to him as a gift.... It is the Holy One, blessed be He, who leads man in the path he has chosen, and who imparts to him some of His own holiness, thereby rendering him holy. The man who is holy, he who is always in communion with his God ... is accounted as though he beheld the presence of the Lord, notwithstanding that he is still in this world.[19]

Judaism as well as Christianity and Islam are sometimes characterized as religions of faith, in contrast to Asian religions, which are said to be religions of experience. It is claimed that the Jew is required only to have faith in God and God's revelation. A reading of Luzzatto reveals that the saint not only has faith but that he has real experiences of God in this life. Luzzatto claims that faith in God combined with the will to holiness can lead one step by step "until there is poured upon him a spirit from on high and the name of the Creator, blessed be He, will abide within him as it does within all holy things" (*MY* 452).

Like the Buddhist eight-fold path, Luzzatto's path begins with watchfulness and, as one continues to struggle on this path, one may reach the stage of fear of sin. When one reaches that stage, the Holy Spirit may then descend and one attains holiness. Once one is granted holiness by God, claims Luzzatto, one has the power to resurrect the dead.

Mesillat Yesharim became an important ethical text for both the Mithnagdim and the Hasidim. The Hasidim, who elevated prayer over Torah study and made *devekut* (communion with God) their central goal, felt a strong affinity for Luzzatto's holy path, because they felt it leads to *devekut*. At the same time, the Gaon of Vilna is said to have stated that he could not find a superfluous word in the first seven chapters of *Mesillat Yesharim*—and were Luzzatto still alive, he would walk across Europe to study with him.

But Luzzatto's greatest influence was among the devotees of the Musar movement, an ethical self-perfection movement founded in Vilnius by Rabbi Israel Salanter (1810–1883). Salanter, one of

---

19. Ibid., 444–46.

the most influential Orthodox thinkers of the nineteenth century, felt a strong affinity for Luzzatto, stressing that the primary goal of a human being is to strive for ethical perfection. Rabbi Dov Katz, a third-generation disciple of Salanter, wrote: "His avowed aim in life was the attainment of spiritual perfection. He regarded ethical perfection as the entire purpose for being on earth."[20] Salanter believed that "It was more difficult to change a single character trait than to cover the entire Talmud."[21] Yet for him this was a task that must be undertaken and that would ultimately lead to the transformation of the individual:

> Yet let no one say: What God has made cannot be changed. He, may He be blessed, has infused an evil drive in me; how can I ever hope to eradicate it? It is not so. Man's drives can be subdued and even changed. ... It is within his power to conquer his evil nature and prevent its functioning, and also to change his nature to good by study and training.[22]

In the preface to his book *Mesillat Yesharim* Luzzatto complains that people are devoting too much time to the study of Jewish law and are not paying sufficient attention to the study of Musar: "There are but few who study the nature of the love and the fear of God, of communion, or any other phase of saintliness."[23] This captures precisely the view of Salanter, who made the study of Musar texts central to achieving a holy life and who helped Luz-

20. Katz, *The Musar Movement*, 138.

21. Ibid., 120.

22. As quoted by Dov Katz in *Musar Movement*, 65. It is beyond the scope of the present essay to compare and contrast the holy person in Judaism and Buddhism. However, I do want to point out that a study of the methods of training advocated by the Buddha and Israel Salanter reveals some striking similarities. For example, both advocate meditation on death. I also find it quite striking that Salanter, like the Buddha, believes in the possibility of a radical transformation of the human being. Salanter's closest disciple, Rabbi Simcha Zissel Ziv of Kelm, Lithuania, taught "Take time, be exact, unclutter the mind." He also said, "The worst thing that can happen to a person is to remain asleep and untamed." I see these statements as central teachings of the Buddha.

23. Luzzatto, *MY,* 4.

zatto's *Mesillat Yesharim* become the most widely used basic text among the *Yeshivot* of Lithuania.[24]

At the beginning of the twenty-first century, there are only a few *yeshivot* in the United States and Israel that emphasize Musar in their curriculum. Although there are four English translations of *Mesillat Yesharim*, the Jewish world as a whole is not familiar with the Musar movement and its preeminent ethical text.[25]

A Jewish saint of the twentieth century

Today there is a new, beautiful, ethical text that is capturing the minds and hearts of Jews and members of other faiths throughout the world, especially in America. This work, *God in Search of Man: A Philosophy of Judaism*, was first published in 1955 by Rabbi Abraham Joshua Heschel. I, along with many other Jews and Christians, consider Heschel to be the Jewish saint of the twentieth century. His first student in America, Rabbi Samuel Dresner, claimed that Heschel was "*zaddik hador*," the saint of our generation.[26] For Heschel's disciple Byron Sherwin "Abraham Joshua Heschel was a jewel from God's treasure chest."[27] Christians speak of Heschel as the most significant spiritual writer of our time and often call him a prophet.[28] I view Heschel's *God in Search of Man* as a modern

24. Rabbi Norman Lamm, the former president of Yeshiva University in New York City, reminds us of the great popularity of *MY*. He writes: "Its wide popularity can be gauged by the fact that it was reprinted no less than sixty-six times in a period of one hundred and fifty-five years." *Torah; Lishmah*, 338.

25. The Musar movement had its greatest strength in Lithuania, where 95 percent of the Jews were killed during the Holocaust. Fortunately, a few students from the yeshiva in Slabodka, which was known as "the mother of yeshivas," and from the yeshiva of Volzhin, managed to survive. In *Climbing Jacob's Ladder: One Man's Rediscovery of a Jewish Spiritual Tradition*, Alan Morinis, a secular Jew and a Rhodes scholar who was a professor of Asian religions, tells the incredible story of his meeting with Rabbi Yechiel Yitzchok Perr, a great contemporary Musar teacher and how his life was transformed by this encounter.

26. Dresner, "Heschel," 30.

27. Sherwin, *Abraham Joshua Heschel*, 1.

28. For example, Reinhold Niebuhr spoke of Heschel as "the most

equivalent of Luzzatto's Jewish path to holiness. Heschel's book can be seen as "a way of developing sensitivity to God and attachment to His presence" (*GSM* 26).

God in Search of Man is devoted to three interrelated aspects of a Jewish path through which contemporary Jews can open themselves to God or, more precisely, through which we can respond to God, who according to Heschel, needs human beings. In Heschel's words, "There are three starting points of contemplation about God; three trails that lead to Him. The first is the way of sensing the presence of God in the world, in things; the second is the way of sensing His presence in the Bible; the third is the way of sensing His presence in sacred deeds" (*GSM* 31).

Heschel has been called the philosopher of wonder because he believed that awareness of the divine begins with wonder. For Heschel radical amazement can help us to experience the realm of the ineffable. Heschel takes as his task in the first path to tell us how to sense wonder and awe, how to see the holy in the everyday, to see that all of life is sacred.

The second of Heschel's paths to God is encountering God through the words of the Bible. Heschel asserts that the Bible is the ideal path through which Jews can encounter God. However, mere biblical study will not disclose the presence of God. We must approach the Bible with our whole being. We must also cultivate certain virtues, such as humility and truthfulness, and attempt to rid ourselves of pride, pettiness, and falsehood.

In Heschel's third path, the way of sensing God's presence in sacred deeds, he claims that modern human beings who have difficulty with the first two paths, who still can't open their eyes, have a final alternative. Heschel presents a most challenging and provocative claim. He contends that performing the *mitzvot*, the

---

authentic prophet of religious life in our culture" as quoted by Byron L. Sherwin in "Abraham Joshua Heschel," 7. Heschel's friend Martin Luther King Jr. often spoke of Heschel as a prophet. And at a recent conference in Switzerland, Professor Stanislaw Obirek from Warsaw, Poland, the land of Heschel's birth, called Heschel, "a real prophet." Heschel did not accept being praised as a prophet. He said that he hoped and prayed that he was "worthy of being a descendent of the prophets." See Stern, "Interview," 400.

commandments, is not merely our response to the demands of God. They may also serve as a path *to* God. The fact that contemporary human beings are callous to the mystery of existence and detached from the biblical tradition leads Heschel to say that the way through deeds may be our last hope. The significance that Heschel attaches to sacred deeds becomes apparent when he states, "A Jew is asked to take a leap of action rather than a leap of thought. He is asked to surpass his needs, to do more than he understands in order to understand more than he does. In carrying out the words of the Torah he is ushered into the presence of spiritual meaning. Through the ecstasy of deeds, he learns to be certain of the hereness of God. Right living is a way of right thinking."[29] Farther along, Heschel explains more fully why the Jew is asked to take a leap of action:

> The mitzvah is a supreme source of religious insight and experience. The way to God is a way of God, and the mitzvah is a way of God, a way where the self-evidence of the holy is disclosed.... A mitzvah is where God and man meet.... To meet Him means to come upon an inner certainty of His realness, upon an awareness of His will. Such a meaning, such presence we experience in deeds."[30]

Conclusion

There are clearly major affinities as well as differences between the works of Luzzatto and Heschel. Luzzatto was writing during a time when, for most Jews, God was a reality. His aim was to lead ordinary Jews to saintliness. Heschel, on the other hand, wrote during a time when the belief in a supernatural concept of God was no longer a reality for many Jews. His aim was to convince Jews that awareness of God's reality that would help lead them to a more spiritual, holy life.

29. Ibid., 283.
30. Ibid., 312.

Interfaith Activism

Luzzatto's path is more otherworldly than Heschel's path, with a strong stress on personal transformation. Because of the intense effort that is necessary to attain to saintliness, there is little time in Luzzatto's path for one to be involved in the community. Heschel, on the other hand, is deeply concerned with the everyday. He became involved in a number of compelling social and political issues of his day. He devoted a great deal of time to the Civil Rights Movement, led by Martin Luther King Jr., and to opposing the war in Viet Nam. He also addressed himself to the plight of Jews in the Soviet Union.

Judaism commands love of both God and neighbor. The question that has often been asked is: Does love of God take priority over love of neighbor? I would argue that that is the case for Luzzatto. For Heschel, who always attempted to create a balance between the polarities in Judaism, human beings come first. Heschel observed, "Every human being is made in the image of God. Therefore, if we are serving our fellow human beings, in a very real sense we are serving God as well."[31] This is how Heschel characterized a saint: "A saint was he who did not know how it is possible not to love, not to help, not to be sensitive to the anxiety of others."[32]

With his attention to the world and the divine, Heschel combined the hallowing of the everyday of the Baal Shem Tov with the brilliant scholarship of the Gaon of Vilna and the ethical fervor of Israel Salanter. Heschel described—and lived—a modern path to sainthood.

---

31. Raskas, *Jewish Spirituality*, 9.
32. Heschel, *Earth*, 20–21.

4

Abraham Joshua Heschel: Living with the Holocaust

MY BELOVED TEACHER, ABRAHAM Joshua Heschel, was one of the most important Jewish thinkers of the twentieth century and his influence has only been growing since his death. There are innumerable articles and books on his work, yet very little has been written about his reaction to the Holocaust. This may be because he did not write a separate study on the Holocaust and also because in his written work he had a tendency to stress one point of view and then another point of view. On certain issues, Heschel's perspectives are extremely complex. This seems to be especially the case in writing about the Holocaust. Even today, for example, more than forty years after his death, Heschel scholars are deeply divided on whether he believed in divine omnipotence, a God who is all powerful, and thus whether he believed that God might have been able to prevent the Holocaust from happening.

Although Heschel did not focus directly on the Holocaust, we do find in his writings many statements from which we can discern its profound impact on his life. In a 1967 interview at Notre Dame University he stated: "I am really a person who is in anguish. I can't forget what I have seen and been through. Auschwitz and Hiroshima never leave my mind. Nothing can be the same after that."[1] Heschel further claims that "Auschwitz is in our veins. It abides in the throbbing of our hearts. It burns in our imagination. It trembles in our conscience."[2] In one of his most important essays, "No Religion Is an Island," Heschel defines himself as a survivor: "I am a brand plucked from the fire in which my people was burned to death. I am a brand plucked from the fire of an altar of Satan on which millions of lives were exterminated to evil's greater glory. . . . "[3] We now also know that during Heschel's first five years in America (1940–1945) he made many efforts, unfortunately in vain, to rally support for intervention that would save European Jews. What did he do when no one listened to him? He went to a synagogue to pray, fast, recite psalms, and weep.[4] Like many other survivors, Heschel struggled with God his entire life, a struggle that continued to the very end and, I believe, was never fully resolved. In one of his most extraordinary talks which has been reprinted numerous times, Heschel cried out to God, "Where is God? Why didst Thou not halt the trains loaded with Jews being led to slaughter? It is so hard to rear a child, to nourish and to educate. Why dost Thou make it so easy to kill?" (*MQG*, 148)[5]

On the one hand a reading of Heschel shows that he blamed the Holocaust on humanity: "For the Holocaust did not take place suddenly. It was in the making for several generations. It had its origin in a lie; that the Jew was responsible for all social ills, for all personal frustrations. Decimate the Jews and all problems would be solved. The Holocaust was initiated by demonic thoughts, savage words."[6] Clearly, here, he blames the Holocaust on the depravity of human beings. It was they who created the gas chambers.

A number of Heschel's friends and students were puzzled that he did not write more directly about the Holocaust. Arthur

1. Heschel, "Interview at Notre Dame," 390.
2. Heschel, *Israel*, 206.
3. Heschel, "No Religion," 235.
4. Kaplan, *Spiritual Radical*, 44.
5. Heschel originally expressed these sentiments in 1938 at a conference of Quaker leaders in Frankfurt-am-Meim, Germany.
6. Heschel, *Passion*, 321.

Living with the Holocaust

Green tells us how difficult it was to be a follower of Heschel. At a time when he was reading Elie Wiesel's book *Night*, in which Wiesel speaks of God as dying on the gallows of Auschwitz, and Richard Rubenstein was saying that it was blasphemy to continue to believe in divine providence, Heschel was writing on Jewish ways of encountering God's presence. Emil Fackenheim, who was a great admirer of Heschel, points out that, like Martin Buber, Heschel "said little about the Holocaust—and that little with great reticence."[7] Fackenheim came to understand that Heschel did not formulate a new theology of the Holocaust because it did not pose a new theological problem for him. And Heschel's students came to understand that his stand against the war in Viet Nam, his deep involvement with Martin Luther King, and his action for Soviet Jewry were his response to the Holocaust. Heschel wanted to find ways to help God heal the world rather than to speculate about how to justify God. For Heschel God needs partners; he does not need our recommendation.

Heschel's experience of the Holocaust is certainly one of the reasons for his social activism. He lived in Germany from 1927 to 1938, where he experienced racism and often pointed out how violence towards others begins with words. His daughter Susannah Heschel tells us, "He used to remind us that the Holocaust did not begin with the building of crematoria, and Hitler did not come to power with tanks and guns; it all began with uttering evil words, with defamation, with language and propaganda."[8] Heschel did not blame God. He said that God did not do it. Man did it. For Heschel, God is a God of pathos who cares and participates in human suffering and, therefore, was there with the victims in the Holocaust.

On the other hand, Heschel could not totally give up the idea that God could have intervened in the Holocaust. We are now touching on one of the most critical and controversial issues. There is serious disagreement among scholars as to whether Heschel rejects the idea of divine omnipotence. In his classic work God in

---

7. Fackenheim, *To Mend the World*, 194.
8. Heschel, S., "Introduction," viii.

Search of Man Heschel tells us that God "combines justice with omnipotence" (*GSM* 171). Later in this same work Heschel does not seem to question the omnipotence of God, stating that "the omnipotence of God is not always perceptible" (*GSM* 241). I agree with John Merkle who, when interpreting Heschel's view, says that "God's presence in history should not be understood as God's dominance of history."[9] But I am not convinced that Heschel gave up on the idea that God could intervene in history to help shape its course. Merkle never suggests that Heschel rejects this idea, but he does suggest that Heschel, at least toward the end of his life, came to reject the idea of divine omnipotence. Although he makes a strong case for this, basing his argument upon Heschel's claims that "the idea of divine omnipotence . . . is a non-Jewish idea"[10] and that "God's mercy is too great to permit the innocent to suffer" but that "there are forces that interfere with God's mercy, with God's power,"[11] I believe that Heschel never completely resolved the issue of divine omnipotence.

Heschel, who like many other East European Jews of his time, devoted a good part of his life to the study of the Talmud, the central sacred text of Jewish learning. A core teaching of the Talmud, with which Heschel was certainly familiar, is that "everything is in the hands of heaven except for the fear of heaven" (Berakhot 33b). I fully agree with Gordon Tucker's nonliteral translation of this passage as "God can do anything except make us believe in God."[12] This important passage from the Talmud helps us understand the incredible dilemma that confronted Heschel, who believed in a God of pathos, a God who suffers with the suffering of human beings, who intervened to liberate the children of Israel from

9. Merkle, *Approaching God*, 47–48.

10. Heschel, "Teaching," 160.

11. Heschel, "On Prayer," 260. Merkle lays out his argument most succinctly in *Approaching God*, 47–48, and in note number 71, pp. 100-01, in which he responds to Alexander Even-Chen's article "God's Omnipotence and Presence in Abraham Joshua Heschel's Philosophy" in *Shofar*, edited by Harold Kasimow. For an insightful presentation of Heschel's response to the Holocaust see Kaplan's "Confronting the Holocaust: God in Exile."

12. Tucker, "Heschel," 127.

Egyptian bondage but did not intervene in a similar way during the Holocaust.

For Heschel, as I understand him, the limitation of God's power in history is self-imposed. Heschel's wrestling with God is precisely due to the fact that God does not always interfere in the world during times of great suffering. From the time that Heschel was a young man he confronted God and would not exonerate Him for the world's pain. Human beings are responsible, but that does not let God off the hook from ultimate responsibility. I am still struggling with my last statement because I am aware of Heschel's close affinity to the second century sage, Rabbi Akiva, who "believed that it is better to limit belief in God's power than to dampen faith in God's mercy."[13] However, on this issue I think that Heschel comes closer to the view of Akiva's contemporary, Rabbi Ishmael, who believed in an omnipotent God. Let me explain.

From Heschel's early book of Yiddish poems, *The Ineffable Name of God: Man*, it is clear that Heschel could not adjust himself to the evil in the world. He stands in the tradition of Abraham, of Job, and of his great Hassidic ancestor Levi Yitzhak of Berditchev, who is known for challenging God to bring an end to suffering. In his poem called "Help" Heschel writes:

> The desolate call to You and You don't come.
> So send me, and any others, You might choose.
>
> I can't curse as justly as did Jeremiah.
> People are poor, weak; and it seems to me
> that their guilt is Yours;
> their sins, Your crimes.
>
> You are meant to help here, Oh God!
> But You are silent, while needs shriek.
> So help me to help! I'll fulfill Your duty,
> pay Your debts.[14]

We know that Heschel was deeply influenced by Menahem Mendel, the Kotzker Rebbe. Heschel said: "Throughout my entire

---

13. Heschel, *Heavenly Torah*, 119.
14. Heschel, *Ineffable Name of God*, 33.

Interfaith Activism

life the words of the Kotzker Rebbe burned within me."[15] For Heschel, as for the Kotzker, "A man of flesh and blood was simply not meant to comprehend the divine response to the deepest of human problems. Divine secrets were not compatible with the human intellect."[16] Is there then any purpose in asking these terrifying questions to which we will not get the answers? Both the Kotzker's and Heschel's answer is "Yes." It is true that no answer can be gained by human beings, but we must persist in our search. The Kotzker locked himself up in a room for the last twenty years of his life in order to struggle with God. I'm grateful that Heschel continued his struggle by living among us.

I have spoken of Heschel's responses to the Holocaust, and not his answers, because I agree with the following statement of Elie Wiesel, with which I believe Heschel would concur: "The survivors . . . are aware of the fact that God's presence at Treblinka or Maidanek—or, for that matter, His absence—poses a problem which will remain forever insoluble. . . . Perhaps someday someone will explain how, on the level of man, Auschwitz was possible; but on the level of God it will forever remain the most disturbing of mysteries."[17] Mordecai Kaplan (1881–1983), the great Lithuanian-American philosopher of Judaism who founded the Reconstructionist Movement, had a vision of Judaism that is radically different from Heschel's. Yet when it came to the Holocaust he was in full agreement with Heschel that there is no answer. He said, "Not a single one of the numerous theodicies or attempts of thinkers to reconcile the goodness of God with the existence of evil, has ever proved convincing."[18]

Let me end with a story. "One writer on the Holocaust records that in his researches he met a rabbi who had been through the camps and who miraculously seemed unscarred. He could still laugh. 'How,' he asked him, 'could you see what you saw and

---

15. Heschel, *Kotzk*, 7. This quotation from the Yiddish original is my translation.

16. Heschel, *Passion*, 269.

17. Wiesel, *Legends*, 6.

18. Kaplan, *Questions Jews Ask*, 116.

still have faith? Did you have no questions?' The rabbi replied, 'Of course I had questions. But I said to myself: if you ever ask those questions, they are such powerful questions that God will send you a personal invitation to Heaven to give you the answers. And I preferred to be here on earth with the questions than in Heaven with the answers.' That too is theology of a kind, with roots deep in the biblical tradition."[19]

---

19. Sacks, *Crisis and Covenant*, 41.

5

Swami Vivekananda and Rabbi Abraham Joshua Heschel: Standing on the Shoulders of Giants

> My thesis, therefore, is: no world peace without peace among religions, no peace among religions without dialogue between the religions, and no dialogue between the religions without accurate knowledge of one another.[1]

THIS EXTRAORDINARY STATEMENT BY the Christian theologian Hans Küng must be taken as one of the great challenges for our time if we are to preserve our fragile planet. Küng's assertion that there can be "no world peace without peace among the religions" challenges the religious leaders of the world to interpret their respective traditions in such a way as to encourage spiritual strength that would defeat the violence and destruction, the persecution and intolerance often historically committed in the name of religion. Leaders must face the fact that all religions have brought beauty and astonishing enrichment to millions of believers, but they have simultaneously been the cause of great suffering and anguish because of their exclusive claims to infallibility.

I am convinced that the belief that there can be only one valid religious tradition, only one way to salvation, is a major cause for the hostility between people of different faiths and is the main

---

1. Küng, "Christianity," 194.

obstacle to authentic interfaith dialogue. If religious people are to eradicate the forces of violence and evil and help to bring peace, they must first renounce the exclusivist attitude toward other religions and turn to the vision and wisdom of the spiritual giants of the world's religious traditions. In this essay, I will briefly examine some key ideas of Swami Vivekananda (1863–1902) and Rabbi Abraham Joshua Heschel (1907–1972), focusing on their attitudes toward other religious traditions. I believe that the lives and works of these two spiritual teachers can help to transform our views of other people of faith and thereby help us to mend the world.

Although Vivekananda was a Hindu monist and Heschel was a Jewish theist, I am amazed at the remarkable similarities in their views on many significant issues. Their affinity is particularly striking not only in their views of other religious traditions, but also on such critical issues as the concept of humanity and their vision of God. Let me be very clear that by similar I do not mean identical. The differences are real. But I am convinced that what they have in common is more important than the points on which they differ. And it is that which is more important to be affirmed. By becoming aware of the common elements of these two thinkers, one nurtured in the Hindu tradition and the other in East European Judaism, we are more likely to be open to the spirituality of all people of faith.

Both Vivekananda and Heschel were philosophers and mystics who were critical of certain aspects and doctrines of their own traditions. For Vivekananda and Heschel, theological subtleties were not the most important issues. Their concern was how to save the humanity of human beings. Most important for them was the righteousness of each individual. They both stressed that to attain such a goal one must attempt to experience God in one's own life, to truly come to feel the presence of God. As is clearly shown in the following statement, Vivekananda believed that one can experience the reality of God in one's own life and that such a mystical vision of God is preceded by ethical discipline: "He reveals Himself to the pure heart; the pure and the stainless see God, yea, even in this life. Then all doubt ceases. So the best proof a Hindu sage gives about God is: "I have seen God."[2]

Similarly, Abraham Joshua Heschel, one of the authentic Jewish mystics of the twentieth century, cites the Hebrew Bible as a source of Jewish longing for immediate contact with the divine: "Not all of the people of the Bible are satisfied with *awareness* of God's power and presence. There are those *"that seek Him, that seek Thy face O God of Jacob"* (Ps 24:6). . . . At Sinai, according to legend, Israel was not content to receive the divine words through an intermediary. They said to Moses, "We want to hear the words of our King from Himself. . . . We want to see our King" (*GSM* 28–29). Heschel then quotes from Judah Halevi, the great medieval Jewish poet: "To see the face of my King is my sole desire. I fear none but Him; I revere only Him. Would that I might see Him in a dream! I would continue to sleep for all eternity. Would that I might behold His face within my heart! Mine eyes would never ask to look at anything else" (*GSM* 29). Throughout his works, Heschel speaks of the divine-human encounter, of the possibility to experience the presence of God. Certainly Heschel, the theist, and Vivekananda, the monist, describe the mystical experience differently. However, both would agree that what is most important is the transformation that is brought about by this experience. For both, the key is "to forget the self," and by so doing to experience a tremendous concern for other human beings and the world.

For Vivekananda and Heschel, saving the world seems to be more central than personal salvation. In fact, personal salvation is undertaken only as a means to save the world. Throughout his writings, Vivekananda emphasizes the divine nature of human beings. According to him, the central aim of man and woman lies in "aiding humanity to realize its own true, divine nature."[3]

This emphasis is also found in the thought of Heschel. He insists that the fundamental statement about human beings, according to the Jewish tradition, is found in the following passage in Genesis: "And God said, 'I will make man in My image, after

2. Nikhilananda, *Vivekananda*, 185.
3. Embree, *Hindu Tradition*, 322.

My likeness . . .' And God created man in His image, in the image of God He created him; male and female He created them" (Gen 1:26–27). Heschel interprets this statement as follows:

> The intention is not to identify "the image and likeness" with a particular quality or attribute of man, such as reason, speech, power or skill. It does not refer to something which in later systems was called "the best in man," "the divine spark," "the eternal spirit" or "the immortal element" in man. It is the whole man and every man who was made in the image and likeness of God. It is both body and soul, sage and fool, saint and sinner, man in his joy and in his grief, in his righteousness and wickedness. The image is not in man; it is man.[4]

I am not attempting to blur the distinction between Vivekananda the Hindu monist and Heschel the Jewish theist. In the Jewish tradition, a human being is never divine. But what stands out for me is the preciousness of human beings that emerges in the works of these two thinkers.

The keystone for both Vivekananda and Heschel is love of God and love and compassion for human beings. God is central, but both stress that this love must be manifested in love for human beings. Vivekananda states that "the gist of all worship: to be good and to do good to others"[5] and that "each is responsible for the evil anywhere in the world."[6] Similarly Heschel claims that "only a free person knows that the true meaning of existence is experienced in giving, in endowing, in meeting a person face to face, in fulfilling other people's needs" (*MNA* 214) and that "some are guilty, all are responsible."[7] Here is where their affinity is strongest. Both strongly agree that religion cannot be separated from social and political issues. In order to bring about the kingdom of God on earth and beautify all parts of our globe, love of God must manifest itself in love for all human beings.

4. Heschel, *"Concept of Man,"* 128.
5. Nikhilananda, *Vivekananda*, 198.
6. Ibid., 197.
7. Heschel, "Moral Outrage," 50.

Interfaith Activism

I first encountered Swami Vivekananda in a course that I took with Bernard Phillips at Temple University in Philadelphia. During the first few weeks of my study of the Hindu tradition, I was moved by a statement that Vivekananda made at the World Parliament of Religions on September 11, 1893: "I am proud to belong to a religion which has taught the world both tolerance and universal acceptance. We not only believe in universal toleration, but we accept all religions as true."[8] I felt a strong affinity for this view. This may seem surprising in view of the fact that I was raised in an East European, traditional Jewish family. My education was also very traditional. When I arrived with my family in the United States at the age of twelve, I studied at Yeshiva Salanter, and then at Talmudical Academy of Yeshiva University. My Jewish education continued at the Jewish Theological Seminary and at the University of Jerusalem. During all those years, we never discussed the major faiths of other human beings. Yet even at that time, I had problems with the traditional Jewish view that Judaism is the only authentic religious tradition.

Although I would not have expressed it in this way, I found it problematic even then that God could be approached only through the Torah. Today, after more than thirty years of study of other religious traditions and being immersed in my own tradition, I find it even more difficult to agree with Jews who are convinced that ours is the superior path. Why not think of ourselves as seekers who are fortunate to belong to a rich tradition that is able to be even more enriching as we learn more deeply of the spiritual life of a tradition other than our own? Isn't it enough to know that we follow Judaism, not because it is superior, but because it is ours? Since it is clear that the concept of the chosen in any of the traditional Jewish sources has never meant that Jews are better than anyone else, why isn't it possible to understand the concept of the chosen in terms of God choosing the Jews to follow the path of the Torah, and at the same time, choosing the Hindus to follow the Vedas, the Muslims to follow the Qur'an, and for Christians to follow Jesus of Nazareth?

8. Nikhilananda, *Vivekananda*, 183.

I was also very moved by Vivekananda's statement at the final session of the World Parliament of Religions on September 27, 1893: "If the Parliament of Religions has shown anything to the world, it is this: it has proved to the world that holiness, purity, and charity are not the exclusive possessions of any church in the world, and that every system has produced men and women of the most exalted character."[9] I was drawn by this statement not only to seek a deeper knowledge of Eastern religions but to see if there is anything in my own tradition that would support this view which I found so enticing. I began by rereading the works of my teacher Abraham Joshua Heschel and was struck by his statement that Judaism could be enriched if dialogue would occur "between the River Jordan and the River Ganges." Heschel was one of the few Jews that I had ever met who believed that it was "vitally important . . . for Judaism to reach out into non-Jewish culture in order to absorb elements which it may use for the enrichment of its life and thought . . ." (*GSM* 15).

Soon after, I decided that I would write my PhD dissertation on Heschel. During the summer of 1972, I presented him with my proposed dissertation topic, part of which would compare his thought to *bhakti yoga*, the Hindu path of love. Heschel's response after reading my proposal was "a fine outline, a good promise." Although my completed dissertation did not include this comparative aspect of Heschel and the Hindu path of love, I certainly came to see the Jewish stream of thought which is in full agreement with Vivekananda's statement that all traditions produce saints.

It would be inaccurate to suggest that Jewish scholars have totally ignored the idea that saints arise outside of the Jewish tradition. Rabbi Jacob Agus, who was a frequent participant in interfaith dialogue, finds rabbinic sources that support the idea that there may have been Gentile prophets who were greater than Moses.[10] But somehow Jews have forgotten to stress this idea; one that I believe holds great promise for future interreligious dialogue because it can move us away from an exclusivist position. With the

9. Ibid., 197.
10. Agus, "Context and Challenge," 38.

Jewish idea that saints are produced everywhere, we must not limit Jewish dialogue to Christians and Muslims, but we must also reach out to Hindus and Buddhists. If Bahya ibn Pakuda and Abraham Maimonides, two of the most influential medieval Jewish writers, enriched the Jewish tradition through their study of Islamic mysticism, will not contemporary Jewish thinkers also be enriched by the study of important Hindu thinkers such as Vivekananda?

In his inaugural address delivered at Union Theological Seminary in 1965, Heschel presented a view of the religions of the world that was fully in the spirit of tolerance expressed by Vivekananda at the World Parliament of Religions. Heschel asserted: "Perhaps it is the will of God that in this aeon there should be diversity in our forms of devotion and commitment to Him. In this aeon diversity of religions is the will of God."[11] Here Heschel seems to leave little doubt that Jews, Christians, and Muslims, in their various ways, are truly worshipping God. But would this statement apply to other world religions whose concept of God is totally different from that of the Jewish tradition? Heschel quotes a passage from the prophet Malachi and follows it with an interpretation which indicates that Eastern traditions are also valid to him:

> For from the rising of the sun to its setting My name is great among the nations, and in every place incense is offered to My name, and a pure offering; for My name is great among the nations, says the Lord of Hosts (Mal 1:11). This statement refers undoubtedly to the contemporaries of the prophet. But who were these worshippers of One God? At the time of Malachi there was hardly a large number of proselytes. Yet the statement declares: All those who worship their gods do not know it, but they are really worshipping Me. It seems that the prophet proclaims that men all over the world, though they confess different conceptions of God, are really worshipping One God, the Father of all men, though they may not be aware of it.[12]

11. Heschel, "No Religion," 126.
12. Ibid., 127.

It appears to me that Heschel's understanding of Malachi comes very close to the spirit of Vivekananda exemplified in the following statement made by his guru Sri Ramakrishna: "Supposing it *is* a mistake to worship God in the image—doesn't he know he alone is being worshipped? He will certainly be pleased by that worship."[13]

Heschel's interpretation of the Hebrew Bible in such a way as to bring it in harmony with his idea that religious pluralism is the will of God not only has created a rich atmosphere for Jewish-Christian dialogue but also has opened the door to Jewish encounters with Eastern traditions.

Since Heschel's death in 1972, his pluralistic perspective on other faiths has found support among outstanding Jewish thinkers, including a few seminal Orthodox rabbis of our time. Rabbi Irving Greenberg has recently stated: "Any claim that one understanding of God is the *definitive*, superior one is a form of idolatry."[14] He goes on to say, "God, too, has many messengers. Pluralism leads me to recognize that the overflowing love of the Divine is never exhausted. My presence, my mind, my revelation, no matter how great, cannot exhaust infinity."[15] Rabbi David Hartman, the well-known Orthodox philosopher, adds his powerful voice in presenting a vision of other religious traditions that is consistent with Heschel's view. Hartman believes that a critical task for Jewish thinkers today is to show that one can be a passionate, committed Jew without holding that Judaism is the only true religion:

> We must aspire to develop religious forms of commitment and passion that do not require believing that only one tradition reflects the truth. The vitality of religious commitment is not necessarily a function of exclusivity

---

13. Isherwood, *Ramakrishna*, 264. We need not be surprised, therefore, that the Center for Integrative Education, whose "main areas of interest have been the mediation of Eastern and Western thought," realized the affinity between Heschel and Eastern thought and asked him to become a member of their Board of Correspondents. A copy of this letter, dated June 9, 1972, was given to me by Rabbi Heschel.

14. Greenberg, *Religions in Dialogue*, 30.

15. Ibid., 34.

and uniqueness. The presence of other religious traditions need not threaten a person's total devotion and commitment to a particular tradition. Affirmation does not entail the de-legitimization of 'the other.'[16]

In his remarkable book *The Dignity of Difference: Avoiding the Clash of Civilizations*, Jonathan Sacks, Chief Rabbi of Britain and the Commonwealth, makes a most profound case for a pluralistic view that also emerges from the writings of Heschel. The book was written as a response to the tragic events of September 11, 2001, after his visit to Ground Zero with other religious leaders and reflecting on the power of religion as a force for good and evil. Sacks believes that "men kill because they believe they possess the truth while their opponents are in error." For Sacks, as for Greenberg and Hartman, "Truth on earth is not, nor can it aspire to be, the whole truth.... In heaven there is truth; on earth there are truths."[17] In the spirit of Heschel and in words that are almost identical, Sacks writes "that the truth at the beating heart of monotheism is that God is greater than religion; that he is only partially comprehended by any faith."[18]

Heschel's view of other faiths and his call for a meeting "between the river Jordan and the river Ganges" is being carried out today by Alon Goshen-Gottstein, the Orthodox rabbi who directs the Elijah School for the Study of Wisdom in World Religions. The Elijah School brings together scholars and spiritual leaders of the major faiths for interfaith dialogue. The school was founded on the belief that "all religions are in some ways instruments of the divine."[19] The Elijah School is committed to teaching the wisdom of the three Abrahamic faiths as well as the wisdom of the Asian traditions so that we can hear the voice of Rabbi Heschel as well as the voice of Swami Vivekananda.

---

16. Sacks, "Religious Diversity and the Millenium," internet article at www.hartmaninstitute.com, (2001), 2.
17. Sacks, *Dignity*, 64.
18. Ibid., 65.
19. Goshen-Gottstein, "Jewish-Christian Relations, 6.

Jewish and Hindu sages were aware from early times that there were different paths to God. Yet it seems to me that what was critical to many of them, as it is for Vivekananda and Heschel, was not which religious path an individual follows, but how human he or she really is. What is most significant is not the religion of an individual but how pious the individual is. I would contend that the idea that the individual life of each human being is of greater significance than one's own particular religious tradition is at the heart of the teaching of both Heschel and Vivekananda.

In my judgment, both Vivekananda and Heschel were genuine spiritual teachers who have much to say to us today regarding tolerance for different religious traditions. Both argued that what is most important is the struggle to experience God, which leads to being truly human. What is most critical for them is the ethical quality of a person's life.

Thus it was Vivekananda who not only helped me to understand the spirit of tolerance in the Hindu tradition but also led me to see that this spirit of tolerance is present in my own tradition. For this I am very grateful to him.

6

You Are My Witnesses: Maurice Friedman and Abraham Joshua Heschel[1]

ACCORDING TO THE BAAL Shem Tov, the founder of Hasidism, all our encounters with other human beings hold great significance. The truth of this teaching is borne out in my own life by the profound effect that two remarkable men have had on me: Maurice Friedman and Abraham Joshua Heschel. I want to express infinite gratitude to these two witnesses for *Tikkun olam*, literally "the perfecting of the world." *Tikkun olam* is the belief that human beings share a great deal of power with God in bringing about a real transformation in the world that is created and ruled by God. Both Friedman and Heschel are aware of the imperfection of the world, but both refuse to adjust to the falsehood and vulgarity in it. They speak out strongly against the emphasis which contemporary American culture places on success and power. Heschel was and Friedman continues to be passionate and articulate champions of human rights in pursuit of peace and justice for all people.[2]

---

1. The title for this essay is from Maurice Friedman's book *Abraham Joshua Heschel and Elie Wiesel: You Are My Witnesses*.

2. See the contributions of both Heschel and Friedman to Polner's *The Challenge of Shalom*.

In this essay I will focus on Friedman's and Heschel's attitudes toward other religions. I am convinced that our perspectives on other religious traditions play a major role in hindering or promoting peace and justice. Interfaith dialogue and peace go together. Interfaith dialogue is imperative in our time because it is a path to creating a world of greater understanding, thereby helping to eradicate prejudice and intolerance. I take very seriously the following statement on peace and interfaith dialogue by the Christian theologian Hans Küng, "My thesis, therefore, is: no world peace without peace among religions, no peace among religions without dialogue between the religions, and no dialogue between the religions without accurate knowledge of one another.[3]

This extraordinary statement must be taken as one of the great challenges for our time if we are to preserve our fragile planet. Küng's assertion that there can be "no world peace without peace among religions" challenges the religious leaders of the world to interpret their respective traditions in such a way as to encourage spiritual strength that would defeat the violence and destruction, the persecution and intolerance often committed in the name of religion. Leaders must recognize that all religions have brought beauty and astonishing enrichment to millions of believers, but they have also been the cause of great suffering and anguish because of their claims of infallibility.

I am convinced that the belief that there is only one valid religious tradition is a major cause for the hostility between people of different faiths and is a main obstacle to authentic interfaith dialogue. If religious people are to eradicate the forces of violence and evil—even among their own people—and help to bring peace, they must first renounce the exclusivist attitude toward other religions and turn to the vision and wisdom of the spiritual giants of the world's religious traditions. I believe that the works and actions of Maurice Friedman and Abraham Joshua Heschel, two extraordinary teachers, can move us in the direction of greater concern for each other, of confirming one another in our uniqueness.

---

3. Küng, "Christianity," 194.

Interfaith Activism

In my study of the religious traditions of the world I have found a great deal of similarity in their attitudes toward other faiths; they all move in the direction of exclusivism and triumphalism. This is the case not only with Judaism, Christianity, and Islam, but also with Hinduism and Buddhism. On the whole, the major thinkers in these five religious traditions do not entertain the possibility that other traditions may be just as valid. They all seem to agree that their way is the only true way and that followers of other traditions are in error. In some cases they see the other religions as earlier stages of development. But in most cases these thinkers do not acknowledge that salvation or liberation can be obtained through other faiths.

We are well aware of the Christian view that outside the church there is no salvation and the Muslim view that there is only one authentic God-ordained religious tradition for humanity: the straight path of Islam.[4] We may read in texts that deal with world religions that Asian religions are far more tolerant of other paths. However, in my judgment, one of the most tolerant forms of Hinduism—the Ramakrishna Vivekananda version—nevertheless teaches the superiority of Hinduism. Even other forms of Hinduism such as Bhakti Yoga are seen as earlier stages of spiritual development. It also seems to me that the central thrust of the Buddhist tradition, in spite of its great stress on compassion and wisdom, is that it is the only true path. The way of the Buddha is the only path that leads to true liberation.

Similarly, in my opinion, the most widely held view among Jews throughout the ages is that Judaism is the only true religion. The following statement by Immanuel Jakobovits, the former chief rabbi of Great Britain, can serve as a good example of the contemporary Orthodox attitudes towards other faiths. He writes: "As a professing Jew, I obviously consider Judaism the only true religion. Judaism, to be true to itself, is bound to reject, for instance, the

---

4. For a valuable examination of Christian attitudes toward other religious traditions, see Paul F. Knitter, *Introducing Theologies of Religions*. For Muslim views of other religious traditions, see the works of Sayyid Abul A'la Mawdudi and Seyyed Hossein Nasr.

divinity of Jesus or the prophecy of Mohammed as false claims; otherwise its own claims, such as the supremacy of Moses' prophecy and the finality of Mosaic Law... could not be true. Two mutually exclusive statements of conflicting fact can never be completely true."[5] Rabbi Jakobovits can find support for his position both in the Talmud and among most medieval Jewish thinkers. In his epistle to Yemen, Moses Maimonides, the most influential Jewish thinker of the Middle Ages, wrote: "The difference between our religion and the other denominations that liken themselves to us is like the difference between the living, rational individual and the statue skillfully molded out of marble, wood, silver, or gold that looks like a man."[6]

A number of contemporary rabbis and Jewish scholars involved in interfaith dialogue have centered their attention on the Talmudic doctrine of the Seven Commandments of the Sons of Noah, which state that "the righteous of all nations have a share in the world-to-come." This doctrine is considered a valid basis for granting validity not only to Christianity and Islam but also to other religious traditions. The following statement by Ezra Spicehandler is typical of this view: "Judaism is certainly not the one true religion. Even according to the Talmud, all who observe the Noahide laws have a share in the world to come."[7] Rabbi Ben Zion Bokser argued that "the classic Jewish position that the righteous of all nations and all faiths have a share in the world to come implies the legitimacy of diverse paths to God."[8]

Nevertheless, the fact remains that Jews have accepted the view of Maimonides that it is not enough for the gentile to observe the Noahide laws. He or she must follow these laws because they are commanded by God. I am in full agreement with Paul Van Buren when he states that "Jews are going to have to work out their understanding of the church from their central affirmations of

---

5. Jakobovits, "The Condition," 112–13.
6. Maimonides, "The Epistle," 99.
7. Spicehandler, "The Condition," 232–33.
8. Bokser, "The Bible," 16.

God, Torah, Israel and not out of something as off-to-the-side as the Noahide tradition."[9]

The danger of misusing religion for personal, selfish ends and the danger of claims of infallibility are very troubling to Friedman and Heschel. Both wrestled at length with the issue of religion as a cause of evil in the world. Yet in spite of the evil committed in the name of religion, Friedman and Heschel, true to their tradition, never give up the idea of *tikkun olam*. Their trust in God and love for human beings gives them the strength to continue their work, not for personal salvation, but for the advancement of redemption.[10]

In my judgment, the most promising Jewish view towards a pluralistic world, one that could encourage genuine interfaith relations, is the way of Friedman and Heschel. I speak of the way of Friedman and Heschel because I find a very strong affinity in their views of other religious traditions. I first became aware of this affinity when I was writing my dissertation on Heschel under Friedman's direction.[11] In his unpublished manuscript written in 1986 titled "Abraham Joshua Heschel and Interreligious Dialogue," Friedman confirms his strong affinity for Heschel on this issue:

> On rereading Heschel's essay "No Religion Is an Island," I am astonished at how fully what Heschel says about

---

9. Kogan, "Reply" 31.

10. In view of the negative image of man which they present to us, one may find their stress on redemption rather surprising. One of Heschel's most important premises is that contemporary human beings live in agony and that "the humanity of man is no longer self-evident" (*WM* 25). He writes: "The overriding issue of this hour in the world and Western civilization is the humanity of man. Man is losing his true image and shaping his life in the image of anti-man" in Renewal of Religious Thought, 114. And Heschel warns us that we should not "take lightly man's pronouncements about himself" (*WM* 24.) This view is strongly supported by Friedman, who says that "We cannot deny . . . that no matter how monstrous, misshapen, irrational, and distorted the images of man presented to us by contemporary literature and art may be, they do mirror 'significant aspects of the human condition in our time.'" Friedman, *To Deny Our Nothingness*, 21.

11. Kasimow, *Divine-Human Encounter*, 82. The foreword to this published version of my dissertation was written by Maurice Friedman.

interreligious cooperation corresponds to my own approach to interreligious dialogue via what I call the "dialogue of touchstones." In *The Human Way,* I claim that the only realistic modern approach is that of religious pluralism. This is exactly what Heschel says and in the same spirit of dialogue and even of a dialogue of touchstones.

In the first part of his essay, Friedman quotes approvingly from Heschel's article "No Religion Is an Island." I will therefore present much of Friedman's selection from Heschel so that we can understand as fully as possible both Heschel's and Friedman's views of other faiths.[12]

> Parochialism has become untenable . . . Horizons are wider, dangers are greater . . . *No religion is an island.* We are all involved with one another. Spiritual betrayal on the part of one of us affects the faith of all of us. Views adopted in one community have an impact on other communities. Today religious isolationism is a myth. (345)

> My first task in every encounter is to comprehend the personhood of the human being I face, to sense the kinship of being human, solidarity of being . . . A person is . . . all of humanity in one, and whenever one man is hurt we are all injured. The human is a disclosure of the divine, and all men are one in God's care for man. Many things on earth are precious, some are holy, humanity is holy of holies.
> To meet a human being is an opportunity to sense the image of God, *the presence* of God. (347)

> On the level of faith we experience in one another the presence of a person radiant with reflections of a greater presence. (348)

> The purpose of religious communication among human beings of different commitments is mutual enrichment

---

12. Parenthetical page references in the following passages are to "No Religion Is an Island" as reprinted in Frank Talmadge's *Disputation and Dialogue.*

and enhancement of respect and appreciation rather than the hope that the person spoken to will prove to be wrong in what he regards as sacred.

Dialogue must not degenerate into a dispute, into an effort on the part of each to get the upper hand. (352)

Does not the all-inclusiveness of God contradict the exclusiveness of any particular religion? . . . Is it not blasphemous to say: I alone have all the truth and the grace, and all those who differ live in darkness, and are abandoned by the grace of God?

Is it really our desire to build a monolithic society: one party, one view, one leader, and no opposition? Is religious uniformity desirable or even possible? Has it really proved to be a blessing for a country when all its citizens belonged to one denomination? Or has any denomination attained a spiritual climax when it had the adherence of the entire population? Does not the task of preparing the kingdom of God require a diversity of talents, a variety of rituals, soul-searching as well as opposition?

Perhaps it is the will of God that in this aeon there should be diversity in our forms of devotion and commitment to Him. In this aeon diversity of religions is the will of God. (352-53)

The ultimate truth is not capable of being fully and adequately expressed in concepts and words. The ultimate truth is about the situation that pertains between God and man. "The Torah speaks in the language of man." Revelation is always an accommodation to the capacity of man. No two minds are alike, just as no two faces are alike. The voice of God reaches the spirit of man in a variety of ways, in a multiplicity of languages. One truth comes to expression in many ways of understanding. (353-54)

Holiness is not the monopoly of any particular religion or tradition. Wherever a deed is done in accord with the will of God, wherever a thought of man is directed toward Him, there is the holy. (357)

What then is the purpose of interreligious cooperation? ... [It is] to cooperate in trying to bring about a resurrection of sensitivity, a revival of conscience; to keep alive the divine sparks in our souls, to nurture openness to the spirit of the Psalms, reverence for the words of the prophets, and faithfulness to the Living God. (359)

In a letter written to me on July 17, 1986, accompanying his manuscript on Heschel, Friedman says: "I think no reader can doubt what I say: that we are in astonishing agreement and that what I write is very much in his spirit." In *Touchstones of Reality*, one of his most personal books, Friedman states:

> The reality of pluralism must be the starting-point of any serious modern faith. We should give up looking for the one true religion and consider our religious commitments as unique relationships to a truth which we cannot possess. We should also give up the notion that some men possess the spirit and others do not."[13]

These statements by Friedman and Heschel make it clear that for them no one has a monopoly on God. God is found in human hearts everywhere, not just in the Jewish tradition. What is most critical for Friedman and Heschel is not what religion an individual belongs to but how human he or she is. What is most significant is not the tradition an individual follows but how the individual acts in his or her everyday life in order to enhance the power of human love, the power of peace, and the power of justice.

The affinity between Friedman and Heschel in their approaches to members of other faiths may seem surprising to many who know of Friedman primarily as the friend of and the

---

13. Friedman, *Touchstones*, 214. The last time I saw Rabbi Heschel was on June 13, 1972. He told me how moved he was by Friedman's book Touchstones of Reality, a manuscript of which was on top of one of his piles. I later read a statement that Heschel gave to Friedman's editor at Dutton in which he describes this work as a "deeply moving account of a personal pilgrimage of a highly sensitive and rich soul."

INTERFAITH ACTIVISM

foremost authority on the life and thought of Martin Buber. What is less known is that Friedman was also a friend and near-disciple of Heschel. The relationship between them was one of affection and friendship. In the conclusion to his article, "Abraham Heschel among Contemporary Philosophers," Friedman speaks of his indebtedness to Heschel:

> The evaluations that I have made of Heschel's thought from the standpoint of an American raised in a tradition of liberal Judaism give no adequate indication of my great intellectual and spiritual indebtedness to him in the course of more than a quarter of a century of personal friendship. To Heschel I owe my understanding of prayer, *kavanah*, *hasidut*, wonder and awe, the Psalms as a part of daily living, the Sabbath as a holiday of joy, and many other things Jewish.[14]

As we study the life and thought of Friedman, we begin to see that Heschel became a very important touchstone for him. But Friedman, who wrestled intensely with Heschel's vision of Judaism, could not accept Heschel's view of Jewish law, which was based on a different understanding of revelation. On this critical issue, Friedman's view is much closer to that of Martin Buber. Friedman agrees with Heschel that revelation is a dialogue between the prophet and God and that the prophet is "not a passive recipient" (*GSM* 259). But Friedman did not accept Heschel's stress that the content of revelation is as important as the event of revelation. In his interpretation of Martin Buber's position on Judaism and law, Friedman states that for Buber "the laws of the Bible are only the human response to revelation, and, therefore, are not binding on future generations."[15] I believe that this is also Friedman's own position, which is quite problematic for Heschel, who for many years encouraged Friedman to accept Jewish law (*halakhah*). Although Friedman could not agree with Heschel on this issue, the

---

14. Friedman, "Heschel among Contemporary Philosophers," 303.
15. Friedman, "Martin Buber," 1433.

friendship between these two Jewish philosophers lasted for nearly thirty years, until Heschel's death on December 23, 1972.[16]

I first met Maurice Friedman in 1968 when I enrolled in his course on Jewish and comparative mysticism. For this course, I wrote my first paper on Heschel, one titled "Mystical Elements in the Thought of Abraham Joshua Heschel." I also wrote a review essay on Martin Buber's "The Place of Hasidism in the History of Religion" in which Buber compares Hasidism with Zen Buddhism.[17] I certainly did not have the faintest idea at that time that thirty-five years later I would still be immersed in such a study.[18] At that time, however, I was very taken by Buber's tales and wrote a paper titled "My Encounter with the Hasidic Tales" for the literature and existentialism course which Friedman offered in the fall of 1969.

My favorite Hasidic tale is the story of Eizik, son of Rabbi Yekel, who travels from Krakow to Prague in search of treasure. He ultimately discovers, after meeting with a Christian, that the treasure is in fact buried in his family's home in Krakow. Thus, it is a member of a different religious tradition who helps Rabbi Eizik to find the treasure in Judaism, to perceive more profoundly the depth and the uniqueness of the Jewish tradition. Friedman, in his interpretation of this tale, states:

> Perhaps if we had not gone to "Prague," we should not have discovered that the treasure was hidden beneath our own hearth. There is meaning in our searching, even when it takes us far afield, if it enables us to come back home to the unique task which awaits us ... This was my own experience in relation to Judaism. Brought up in a liberal Judaism of a very thin variety, I could never have returned to Judaism and established a new and deeper relationship with it had I not gone through Hinduism, Buddhism, Zen, Taoism, and Christian mysticism. Nor

---

16. For a detailed account of the great affection that developed between Friedman and Heschel, see chapter one "My Friendship with Abraham Joshua Heschel" in Friedman's book *Abraham Joshua Heschel and Elie Wiesel*.
17. Buber, "The Place," 219–39.
18. Kasimow et al. *Beside Still Waters*.

have I lost these other touchstones. They are part of the way in which I came to Hasidism and relate to it.[19]

Friedman, who was deeply influenced by the Hebrew Bible, Hasidic spirituality, Buber, and Heschel, and who considered himself to be a neo-Hasid, was also deeply touched by other religious traditions. As I write this essay, I realize that a number of the crucial touchstones of reality for Friedman have also become touchstones of reality for me.

I was born a few years before the Nazi occupation in a small village near Vilna in a traditional Orthodox Jewish family, although my mother's family belonged to the Lakhovich-Koidanov Hasidic dynasties of Lithuania. My education was also very traditional. When I arrived with my family in the United States after the war in 1949, I studied at Yeshiva Salanter, and then at Talmudical Academy of Yeshiva University. My Jewish education continued at the Jewish Theological Seminary and at the University of Jerusalem. Today, after nearly thirty-five years of study of other religious traditions and having participated in a number of meditation retreats under the direction of Zen Buddhist masters in the U.S., Canada, and Japan, I believe that I have developed a deeper understanding of and attachment to my own tradition. Although I consider myself to be a committed Jew, I am also a pluralist deeply influenced by both Friedman and Heschel. The Jewish tradition is my tradition, the one which is most precious to me, but I do not believe that it is the only valid religious tradition. I am firmly convinced that the Jewish tradition is not incompatible with religious pluralism. As I come to the conclusion of this tribute to my teacher and friend Maurice Friedman, I am aware that I am even more indebted to him than I have ever realized.

---

19. Friedman, *Touchstones*, 169–70.

7

Prophetic Voices: Abraham Joshua Heschel's Friendship with Martin Luther King Jr.

DURING THE THREE DECADES that Abraham Joshua Heschel lived in the United States (1940–1972), he formed deep friendships with some of the most eminent clergy and academics of his generation. Heschel was especially close to Reinhold Niebuhr, one of the most influential Protestant thinkers of the twentieth century. Ursula Niebuhr claims that "for the last twelve years or so of his life, Abraham really was my husband's closest friend."[1] Heschel was also close to the Reverend William Sloane Coffin, the charismatic Protestant preacher, and Daniel Berrigan, the Jesuit priest and poet. Berrigan said that "Heschel was a father to me. . . . He was a saint."[2] Heschel also developed a deep friendship with Thomas Merton, the most influential American Catholic monk of the twentieth century. Merton wrote that Heschel "is the most significant spiritual writer in this country at the moment. I like his depth and his realism. He knows God."[3] But Heschel's best-known and perhaps most historically important friendship was with Martin

1. Niebuhr, "Notes," 37.
2. Berrigan, *To Dwell*, 179.
3. Merton, *Turning*, 61–62.

Interfaith Activism

Luther King Jr. Heschel believed that King truly represented the spirit of the Hebrew prophets:

> Where in America do we hear a voice like the voice of the prophets of Israel? Martin Luther King is a sign that God has not forsaken the United States of America. God has sent him to us. His presence is the hope of America. His mission is sacred, his leadership of supreme importance to every one of us.[4]

In turn, Dr. King had a deep appreciation for Heschel. He spoke of Heschel as "one of the persons who is relevant at all times, always standing with prophetic insight to guide us through these difficult days."[5] King viewed Heschel as a messenger of God because Heschel's words, "to think of man in terms of white, black, or yellow is more than an error. It is an eye disease, a cancer of the soul,"[6] expressed King's own view for the world.

Indeed, Heschel may have played a major role in influencing King to oppose the Vietnam War.[7] In 1965, Heschel was one of the founders of Clergy and Laity Concerned about Vietnam. Heschel spoke out against the war on January 31, 1967, in Washington, DC: "At this hour Vietnam is our most urgent, our most disturbing religious problem, a challenge to the whole nation as well as a challenge to every one of us as individuals. . . . Vietnam is a personal problem. To speak about God and remain silent on Vietnam is blasphemous."[8] Two months after Heschel's speech, on April 4, 1967, King gave one of his most controversial speeches, "Beyond Vietnam: A Time to Break Silence," at Riverside Church in New York City. Heschel was on the podium with King that day.

After King's tragic assassination, Heschel spoke with Harold Flender about his friend:

---

4. Heschel, "Conversation," 1.
5. King, "Conversations," 2.
6. Heschel, "Religion and Race," 87.
7. Sherwin, *Heschel*, 6.
8. Heschel, "The Moral Outrage," 49.

Prophetic Voices

> Yes, Dr. King was a close friend. I, myself, felt dedicated to his movement and to his ideas. I think he was one of the greatest prophetic spirits we had in this century. He brought great blessing to the world, and it is a great loss to America and to the world—to all of us concerned with the rights of man—that this man was so tragically eliminated from our midst. But he remains a blessing and he continues to be an inspiration. If there is anything in the world I could do to advance the appreciation of his ideas in our time, I will certainly be ready to do so, and I am trying to perpetuate the great legacy of this man.[9]

But what unites these two men beyond their shared respect for each other? What do they have in common? What links their thought?

First and foremost they share a desire to bring about a radical spiritual transformation of humanity. The central problem for them is not the survival of religion but the survival of human beings. Heschel states: "What is needed is a spiritual revolution."[10] Similarly, in his speeches King called for "a revolution in values."

Looking at the role of religion in human history, Heschel and King found that religion has not always been a force for freedom, justice, and peace. Heschel stated:

> Religion as an institution, the Temple as an ultimate end, or, in other words, religion for religion's sake, is idolatry. The fact is that evil is integral to religion, not only to secularism. Parochial saintliness may be an evasion of duty, an accommodation to selfishness.
>
> Religion is for God's sake. The human side of religion, its creeds, rituals and institutions, is a way rather than the goal. The goal is "to do justice, to love mercy and to walk humbly with God." When the human side of religion becomes the goal, injustice becomes a way. (*MNA* 236–7)

---

9. Flender, "Conversation," 3.
10. Heschel, "White Man," 107.

King was also critical of what he saw as serious distortions of religion. In his sermon "Transformed Nonconformist," speaking on the problem of conformity to the world, he states:

> Nowhere is the tragic tendency to conform more evident than in the church.... The mere fact that slavery, racial segregation, war and economic exploitation have been sanctioned by the church is fit testimony to the fact that the church has more often conformed to the authority of the world than to the authority of God.[11]

Yet in spite of the evil committed in the name of religion, Heschel and King did not give up on their traditions. They never forsook the idea that religion is the way to heal the world; that religion can be a way to bring about peace. Heschel could have been speaking for King when he said, "What is needed at this very moment is to mobilize all human beings for one great task, to achieve world peace."[12]

Both felt that religious exclusivism was a major threat to the peace of the world. The common belief among pious people that there is only one valid religion can lead to hatred and violence and even war against the other, the stranger, the member of a different religious tradition. At minimum it is a great obstacle to authentic interfaith dialogue. Both believed that religions working together could become a force for peace. But unfortunately, in the words of Heschel:

> Our terrible sin is not giving peace absolute priority. ... It is conceivable for states to get together and have a United Nations, but it is still inconceivable to have a United Religions.... The situation is very grave.[13]

On this point also King fully agreed with Heschel: "It is not enough to say, 'We must not wage war.' It is necessary to love peace

---

11. King, *Papers*, 472.
12. Heschel, "Choose Life," 255.
13. Ibid., 255–56.

and sacrifice for it. We must concentrate not merely on the eradication of war but on the affirmation of peace."[14]

In his essay "No Religion Is an Island," Heschel presents a radical view of the world's religions. Heschel argues that no religion has a monopoly on truth or holiness and says, "In this aeon diversity of religions is the will of God."[15] For Heschel, "Religion is a means, not an end."[16]

Based on my study of King, he fully supports Heschel's view of other religions. In his 1953 sermon, "Communism's Challenge to Christianity," King said, "historic world religions such as Judaism, Mohammedanism, Buddhism, Hinduism, may be listed as possible alternatives to Christianity . . . ."[17] In *To Make the Wounded Whole: The Cultural Legacy of Martin Luther King, Jr.*, Lewis Baldwin writes that "King held that the personal relationship with God, when examined from the standpoint of the Christian faith, encouraged religious tolerance and a respect for religious pluralism."[18]

For King and Heschel, no religion has a monopoly on God. God is found in human hearts everywhere, not just in one religious tradition. What is most significant is how an individual acts in his or her everyday life to enhance the power of human love, peace, and justice. As men who united a life of prayer with a life of action, they lived their ideal of interreligious dialogue. In his "Letter from Birmingham Jail," which he addressed to Jewish, Catholic, and Protestant clergy, King said, "Too long has our beloved Southland been bogged down in a tragic effort to live in monologue rather than dialogue."[19] A study of King reveals that he was influenced by Martin Buber's vision of dialogue, especially the distinction that Buber made between the *I-It* relationship and the *I-Thou* relationship. With these two interactions in mind King said, "Segregation,

14. King, *Words*, 85.
15. Heschel, "No Religion," 14.
16. Granfield, *Theologians at Work*, 78.
17. King, *Papers*, 147.
18. Baldwin, *To Make*, 145.
19. King, *Why*, 80.

to use the terminology of the Jewish philosopher Martin Buber, substitutes an "I-it" relationship for an "I-Thou" relationship and ends up relegating persons to the status of things. Hence segregation is not only politically, economically, and sociologically unsound, it is morally wrong and sinful."[20]

Heschel and King clearly had similar views on the potential for the corruption of religion, religious pluralism, and the need for interfaith dialogue, but is there a common inspiration for their views? There can be no doubt that Jesus was the major influence on King. But when we compare the talks that King and Heschel each gave at the same conference in 1963, we see that the major theological link between them is reverence for the Hebrew Bible, especially the prophets.

Heschel and King first met at the National Conference on Religion and Race in Chicago in 1963. At this conference, Heschel, "a brand plucked from the fire," who had experienced Nazi racism firsthand, presented one of the most powerful speeches of his life.[21] In his talk, "The Religious Basis of Equality of Opportunity: The Segregation of God," Heschel said that "racism is worse than idolatry. *Racism is Satanism*, unmitigated evil. . . . The aim of this conference is first of all to state clearly the stark alternative. I call heaven and earth to witness against you this day: I have set before you religion and race, life and death, blessing and curse. Choose life."[22] Heschel, who had just recently completed his major work, *The Prophets* (1962), said: "All prophecy is one great exclamation; God is not indifferent to evil! He is always concerned. He is personally affected by what man does to man. He is a God of pathos."[23] To bring about change, Heschel said: "What we need is a total mobilization of heart, intelligence, and wealth for the purpose of love and justice. God is in search of men, waiting, hoping

---

20. Ibid., 82.

21. Byron Sherwin, a disciple of Heschel, writing on the Holocaust, stated that Jews in Nazi Germany "were targeted essentially on racial and not on religious grounds." In "Conceptions," 9.

22. Heschel, "Religious Basis," 56.

23. Ibid., 63.

for man to do His will."²⁴ Although Heschel often stated that the "humanity of man is no longer self-evident" (*WM* 25), he insisted that there is always hope: "The greatest heresy is despair, despair of men's power for goodness, men's power for love."²⁵

In this talk Heschel also presented his concept of man, which he believed to be the core of Judaism. For Heschel the fundamental statement about human beings in the Hebrew Bible is that human beings are created in God's image: "God is every man's pedigree. He is either the Father of all men or of no man. The image of God is either in every man or in no man."²⁶ Heschel ended his talk at Chicago with the following words of the Prophet Amos (5:24): "Let justice roll down like waters, and righteousness like a mighty stream."

Heschel's stress on the sacred image of man, which he believed was the central issue in religious education, is also emphasized in King's speech: "Deeply rooted in our religious heritage is the conviction that every man is an heir to a legacy of dignity and worth. Our Judeo-Christian tradition refers to this inherent dignity of man in the Biblical term *the image of God*."²⁷ This Biblical idea, which was central to Heschel and King, is in my view one of the main motivating forces for their involvement in social action.

Amazingly, toward the end of his speech, King also cites the cry of Amos: "Let justice roll down like waters, and righteousness like an ever flowing stream."²⁸ This is significant. It was Amos who declared that the people of Israel are not more precious to God than the Egyptians, the Philistines, or the Syrians (Amos 9:7). The voice that the Prophet Amos hears tells him that God wants to liberate everyone, not just Jews. Heschel and King looked to the prophets as their models, and therefore they too spoke and acted for the liberation of all people, especially the poor and the oppressed.

24. Ibid., 67.
25. Ibid., 69.
26. Ibid., 66.
27. King, "A Challenge," 158.
28. Ibid., 168.

Interfaith Activism

In her article "Theological Affinities in the Writings of Abraham Joshua Heschel and Martin Luther King Jr.," Susannah Heschel says:

> A comparison of King and Heschel reveals theological affinities in addition to shared political sympathies. . . . Heschel's concept of divine pathos, a category central to his theology, is mirrored in King's understanding of the nature of God's involvement with humanity. For both, the theological was intimately intertwined with the political and that conviction provided the basis of the spiritual affinity they felt for each other.[29]

Her following statement captures the most important affinity between Heschel and King:

> [M]ost striking is the commonality between the spirituality taught by Heschel and King, rooted in the emphasis King gave to the Hebrew Bible and the Exodus narrative and in Heschel's emphasis on the prophets.[30]

Barely five months before his death, King delivered a speech titled "Remaining Awake During a Revolution" at Grinnell College in Iowa, the college at which I have been teaching since 1972. During this historic event for our college, King spoke about his love for all human beings and his concern for the survival of humanity. He gave special stress to the fact that all of life is interrelated and that we must end racial injustice. He repeated the cry of Amos, "Let justice roll down like waters and righteousness like a mighty stream." His core message was that before Amos's statement could become a reality we must realize that "No man is an island, entire of itself." We must talk to each other and be fully present to each other. As King put it "[To] stand alone or live alone in the world today is sleeping through a revolution." King and Heschel were fully awake during the revolution.

---

29. Heschel, "Theological Affinities," 127.
30. Ibid., 129.

8

Did Rabbi Heschel Influence Pope Francis?

By Harold Kasimow and John Merkle

RABBI ABRAHAM JOSHUA HESCHEL is widely known to have had an immense influence on Christians, particularly through his spiritually and theologically penetrating writings that have enriched their understanding of the relationship between God and human beings. As a consequence of this, Heschel inevitably has challenged Christians to rethink traditional Christian teachings about Judaism being an outmoded religion superseded by Christianity. But this challenge has not only been a side effect of Heschel's inspiration to Christians. At times he directly challenged them to develop what he called a "new Christian understanding of Judaism"[1] and "to decide whether Christianity came to overcome, to abolish, or to continue the Jewish way of bringing the God of Abraham and His will to the Gentiles."[2]

Heschel made this direct challenge in a variety of contexts, most notably at the Second Vatican Council (1962–1965), the defining event for Roman Catholicism in the twentieth century,

---

1. Heschel, "From Mission," 9.
2. Heschel, "Jewish Notion," 111.

where he played a prominent role in the negotiations between Jewish organizations and the hierarchy of the Roman Catholic Church. He was the most influential Jewish delegate at the council, encouraging church leaders to condemn anti-Semitism, to eliminate anti-Judaism from church teachings, and to acknowledge the integrity and permanent preciousness of Judaism. By all counts his efforts were hugely successful, as the council's declaration on interfaith relations, *Nostra Aetate* (promulgated on October 28, 1965), signaled a rejection of the traditional supersessionist theology that, for most of Christian history, had marked the church's self-understanding vis-à-vis Jews and Judaism. And not only has this change positively affected Christian-Jewish relations; it also has fostered renewal of Catholic life and theology based on, among other things, a newfound appreciation of the Hebrew Bible, the Jewishness of Jesus and his ministry, and Jewish approaches to God, covenantal life with God, the relationship of the physical and spiritual dimensions of life, and redemption in and of this world.

The influence Heschel had on the Declaration has been widely recognized, as has the fact that his writings have become inspirational reading for countless Christians. But what is perhaps Heschel's most far-reaching, albeit indirect, influence on Christians and Christianity has not previously been noted—i.e., that some of his signature theological ideas appear to have influenced the thinking of the most influential Christian of the early twenty-first century, Pope Francis himself, and that through the pope's teaching these ideas are now reaching a much wider audience than ever before.

Pope Francis never met Rabbi Heschel, and although he is known to own a number of books by Heschel, it is not clear to what extent he has studied Heschel's thought. Nonetheless, it seems that his thinking may have been influenced by Heschel. A few connections between the men point in this direction. Take, for example, the testimony of Rabbi Abraham Skorka of Argentina, one of Pope Francis' closest friends. Rabbi Skorka accompanied Francis on his papal visit to the Holy Land last May (2014), and in 2010 they co-authored the book *On Heaven and Earth*. About the conversations

Did Rabbi Heschel Influence Pope Francis?

that became that book, Rabbi Skorka, who has claimed Rabbi Heschel as a "formative spiritual guide," said that the spirit of Heschel guided their dialogues.³ "We can affirm without any doubt that Heschel's spirit is present in the book we wrote together and in all of our dialogues," Rabbi Skorka explained, "and surely in Pope Francis' attitudes as head of the Catholic Church."⁴

An earlier connection exists through Rabbi Marshall T. Meyer (1930–1993), one of Rabbi Heschel's most devoted students, who became the most influential rabbi in Argentina while the future Pope Francis served as the provincial superior of the Jesuits there and then as rector of the Jesuit university and seminary in San Miguel, outside Buenos Aires. Rabbi Meyer inspired not only Jews but also Christians. He was passionate about spreading Heschel's approach to Judaism and said he felt that Heschel had "accompanied him during his twenty-five years in Argentina.⁵

In light of these connections, we decided to probe what Pope Francis has said and written about topics central to the religious worldview of Rabbi Heschel. We found that Francis has a strong affinity for a number of Heschel's core ideas.

God's search for us

One of Rabbi Heschel's greatest and most influential books is *God In Search of Man: A Philosophy of Judaism* (1955). Like other books of his, it has been translated into Spanish and is widely read not only in Argentina's Jewish community but also by many Argentine Catholics, especially members of the clergy. The title expresses what is perhaps Heschel's most distinctive or signature idea: it is not so much we who seek God, but God who seeks us.

"This is the core of all biblical thoughts," explains Heschel, "God is not a being detached from man to be sought after, but a

---

3. Abraham Skorka in an email message to Alexander Even-Chen, June 16, 2013.

4. Abraham Skorka in an email message to Harold Kasimow, October 24, 2014.

5. Marshall T. Meyer in a letter to Harold Kasimow, June 24, 1987.

power that seeks, pursues and calls upon man. . . . Israel's religion originated in the initiative of God rather than in the efforts of man" (*GSM* 198). By this he does not mean that God does not know where we are and is looking for us. Note what he writes: "God is not a being detached from man." For Heschel, God is always present to us. But because we are not always, or perhaps even usually, present to God, Heschel suggests that God must "reach out" to us (from around us and from within us) to elicit our presence, our responsiveness. We dwell within the sphere of God's presence, yet God must strive to get us to appreciate that presence. God dwells within us, yet God must awaken us to the divine indwelling.

This idea that God searches for us, an idea that Heschel emphasized throughout his adult life, is one that Pope Francis also advances. In his very first entry in chapter one of his book with Rabbi Skorka, Francis states: "I would say that one encounters God walking, moving, seeking Him and allowing oneself be sought by Him. They are two paths that meet. On the one hand, there is our path that seeks Him, driven by that instinct that flows from the heart; and after, when we have encountered each other, we realize that He was the one who had been searching for us from the start."[6] Francis repeated this idea in an interview with Antonio Spadaro, SJ: "We must let God search and encounter us," he said. "God is always first and makes the first move."[7]

God's presence in all people and diverse religions

At the core of Heschel's Judaism is faith in the one God whose search for human beings has received a response from the Jewish people who, by living in a covenant with God, have accepted the challenge of giving witness to God. But just as the biblical and rabbinic authors reminded the people that their being chosen to give this witness to God did not imply either their superiority in relation to other peoples or an exclusive relationship with God,

---

6. Bergoglio and Skorka, *On Heaven and Earth*, 2.
7. Pope Francis, "A Big Heart," 32.

Did Rabbi Heschel Influence Pope Francis?

Heschel points out that it does not imply that the Jewish people are the only vehicle of God's revelation.

According to Heschel, God is, or may be, revealed through each and every human being. "The human is the disclosure of the divine," he said in his inaugural lecture, titled "No Religion Is an Island," as visiting professor at Union Theological Seminary in New York in 1965. "To meet a human being is an opportunity to sense the image of God, the presence of God."[8] Although the Jewish people are chosen for a special type of witness, every human being, created in the image of God, is meant to be "a witness for God," he said elsewhere (*IF* 164). Pope Francis sounded very much like Heschel in the interview he did with Anthony Spadaro, SJ: "God is in every person's life. You can, you must try to seek God in every human life."[9]

While it is a traditional Jewish teaching that every person, created in the image of God, may somehow reveal the presence of God, Heschel goes beyond this in suggesting that Judaism is not the only religion of divine revelation. Speaking specifically about different religious traditions, Heschel insists that divine revelation reaches the human spirit "in a variety of ways, in a multiplicity of languages"[10] and that "God is to be found in many hearts all over the world, not limited to one nation or to one people, to one religion."[11] Pope Francis shows spiritual affinity to Heschel when he writes the following: "God makes Himself felt in the heart of each person. He also respects the culture of all people. Each nation picks up that vision of God and translates it in accordance with the culture, and elaborates, purifies and gives it a system."[12]

In Heschel's view, religions may be considered valid to the extent that they foster awareness of God's love and also love for God and God's creatures. Even non-monotheistic religions may be considered valid to the extent that they foster love for human

---

8. Heschel, "No Religion," 121.
9. Spadaro, *A Big Heart*, 32.
10. Heschel "No Religion," p. 127.
11. Heschel, "Eternal Light," 13.
12. Heschel, *On Heaven and Earth*, 19.

beings, which, for Heschel, "is a way of worshiping God, a way of loving God."[13] Regardless of their theologies, of whether or not they have a monotheistic understanding of ultimate reality, all religions that cultivate such love are, in Heschel's view, valid and vital ways of serving God.

In his lecture at Union, Heschel expressed his belief that "diversity of religions is the will of God."[14] So far, Pope Francis has not spoken explicitly on this issue, so it is uncertain if he would go as far as Heschel on this. In his apostolic exhortation "The Joy of the Gospel," however, Francis seems to offer something in the same spirit as Heschel when he writes: "The same Spirit everywhere brings forth various forms of practical wisdom which help people to bear suffering and to live in greater peace and harmony. As Christians, we can also benefit from these treasures built up over many centuries, which can help us better to live our own beliefs."[15]

The failure of religion

For Heschel, God may be present in and through diverse religions, yet these same religions often fail to manifest God. Here is the opening paragraph of God In Search of Man:

It is customary to blame secular science and anti-religious philosophy for the eclipse of religion in modern society. It would be more honest to blame religion for its own defeats. Religion declined not because it was refuted, but because it became irrelevant, dull, oppressive, insipid. When faith is completely replaced by creed, worship by discipline, love by habit; when the crisis of today is ignored because of the splendor of the past; when faith becomes an heirloom rather than a living fountain; when religion speaks only in the name of authority rather than with the voice of compassion—its message becomes meaningless (*GSM* 3).

---

13. Heschel, *Israel*, 212.
14. Heschel, "No Religion," 126.
15. Pope Francis, "Joy of the Gospel," 122.

Did Rabbi Heschel Influence Pope Francis?

To this summary of Heschel's countless critiques of religion, Pope Francis would surely say "Amen." As a parallel to Heschel's criticism of faith being "replaced by creed" and how "the crisis of today is ignored because of the splendor of the past," Francis' has warned that "faith becomes an ideology among other ideologies" in those who long for "an exaggerated doctrinal 'security,' those who stubbornly try to recover a past that no longer exists."[16] Like Heschel, Francis wants faith to be a "living fountain" rather than an "heirloom." The pope puts it this way: "If the Christian is a restorationist, a legalist, if he wants everything clear and safe, then he will find nothing. Tradition and memory of the past must help us to have the courage to open up new areas to God."[17]

Francis also shares Heschel's criticism of religion when it "only speaks in the name of authority rather than with the voice of compassion." The pope has repeatedly warned against clericalism, for example. "The risk that we must avoid is priests and bishops falling into clericalism, which is a distortion of religion," he explained in his dialogue with Rabbi Skorka. "When a priest leads a diocese or a parish, he has to listen to his community, to make mature decisions and lead the community accordingly. In contrast, when the priest imposes himself, when in some way he says 'I am the boss here,' he falls into clericalism."[18]

Since becoming pope, Francis has denounced clericalism with even greater force. In a closed-door meeting with religious superiors in November 2013, later reported by La Civiltà Cattolica, Francis called clericalism "one of the worst evils."[19] This is reminiscent of Heschel's claim at the convention of the American Medical Association in 1964 that striving for personal success, when it becomes an object of "supreme and exclusive concern," is both "pernicious and demonic" (*IF* 34). And the pope's warning to newly appointed bishops in September 2013, that careerism is

---

16. Spadaro, "Big Heart," 32.
17. Ibid., 32.
18. Bergoglio and Skorka, *On Heaven*, 138.
19. Pope Francis in an address on Nov. 29, 2013, at the Vatican to 120 supervisors of religious orders.

"a form of cancer" sounds just like Heschel's remark in his AMA address: "According to my own medical theory, more people die of success than of cancer."[20]

Rabbi Heschel did not shy away from making harsh criticisms—not of specific people but of what many people do and pursue. Neither does Pope Francis shy away from making such criticisms. But for both men the voice of religion, while necessarily involving prophetic criticism, is ultimately meant to be "the voice of compassion." And for both the rabbi and the pope, interreligious dialogue is urgently needed for people of different traditions to develop that voice and to recognize it in each other.

The urgency of interreligious dialogue

In Rabbi Heschel's view, one of the principal reasons for the failure of religion is the inflation of its importance, treating a given religion as if it were itself divine rather than a human response to the divine. "Religion is a means, not the end," writes Heschel. "It becomes idolatrous when regarded as an end in itself."[21] To assume that there is only one valid way of responding to God is—precisely by absolutizing that way—to equate a religious means with the divine end. About this Heschel is emphatic: "To equate religion and God is idolatry."[22]

For Heschel, genuine monotheistic faith demands an attitude of openness to the validity of various religions precisely because it is opposed to absolutizing—that is, deifying—anything other than God, including a cherished tradition that fosters faith in God. "We must not regard any human institution or object as being an end in itself," writes Heschel. "A temple that comes to mean more than a reminder of the living God is an abomination" (*GSM*, 415). So, contrary to what many people seem to assume, true monotheistic faith means that we must not make our faith the object of our faith.

---

20. Ibid.
21. Heschel, "No Religion," 126.
22. Ibid., 126.

Did Rabbi Heschel Influence Pope Francis?

"There is great merit . . . in our having no absolute faith in our faith," explains Heschel (*GSM* 401). "Human faith is never final, never an arrival, but rather an endless pilgrimage, a being on the way."[23] Therefore, he asserts emphatically: "To rely on our faith would be idol-worship. We have only the right to rely on God" (*MNA* 174).

While Pope Francis has not gone so far as to suggest that reliance on our faith may be a form of idolatry, he has spoken of how faith can be transformed into ideology, which for him is tantamount to idolatry. "The faith passes, so to speak, through a distiller and becomes ideology," Francis said in one of his homilies, and when this happens to the faith of a Christian, he or she becomes "a disciple of ideology." Because "ideologies are rigid, always," and because Christian ideology is "rigid, moralistic, ethical, but without kindness," the pope called this Christian ideology a "serious illness."[24]

For both Heschel and Francis, it is clear that pride and arrogance are at the root of idolatrous and ideological approaches to religion and that the key to genuine religious faith is humility. "A major factor in our religious predicament is due to self-righteousness," Heschel said in his Union lecture. "Religion is often guilty of the sin of pride and presumption. . . . But humility is the beginning and end of religious thinking, the secret test of faith."[25] Speaking about religious ministers, Francis made the same point in his dialogue with Rabbi Skorka: "Humility is what gives assurance that the Lord is there. When someone is self-sufficient, when he has all the answers to every question, it is proof that God is not with him. Self-sufficiency is evident in every false prophet."[26]

Self-sufficiency is also a mark of a false understanding of religion. "The religions of the world are no more self-sufficient, no more independent, no more isolated than individuals or nations," said Heschel. "No religion is an island. We are all involved with

23. Heschel, "No Religion," 128.
24. Pope Francis in a homily at Mass on Oct. 17, 2013, in the chapel of the Vatican's Santa Marta guesthouse.
25. Heschel, "No Religion," 127–28.
26. Bergoglio and Skorka, *On Heaven*, 33.

one another. Spiritual betrayal on the part of one of us affects the faith of all of us. Views adopted in one community have an impact on other communities. Today religious isolationism is a myth."[27] Claiming that "nihilism" is "world-wide in extent and influence," Heschel emphasized the urgency of interfaith dialogue and cooperation: "We must choose between interfaith and inter-nihilism. Cynicism is not parochial. Should religions insist upon the illusion of complete isolation? Should we refuse to be on speaking terms with one another and hope for each other's failure? Or should we pray for each other's health, and help one another in preserving one's respective legacy, in preserving a common legacy?"[28]

Pope Francis takes a similar position. In an address to civic and religious leaders in Brazil in July 2013, Francis emphasized the need for dialogue "in a spirit of openness and without prejudice." He said: "Only in this way can understanding grow between cultures and religions, mutual esteem without needless preconceptions, in a climate that is respectful of the rights of everyone. Today, either we take the risk of dialogue, we risk the culture of encounter, or we all fall; this is the path that will bear fruit."[29]

For both Heschel and Francis, interreligious dialogue is not simply an option but an obligation, because it "is a necessary condition for peace in the world," as Francis writes.[30] Reflecting on the Arab-Israeli conflict, Heschel puts it bluntly: "The choice is to love together or to perish together."[31] And beyond peaceful coexistence, interreligious dialogue also yields spiritual enrichment for those engaged in it. Believing it presumptuous for anyone to think that his or her religion is exclusively true and fruitful, Heschel said in his Union Lecture that "the purpose of religious communication among human beings of different commitments

---

27. Heschel, "No Religion," 119.
28. Ibid., 119.
29. Pope Francis in an address to leading members of Brazilian society on July 27, 2013 (during the week of World Youth Day) in Rio de Janeiro.
30. Pope Francis, *Joy*, 120.
31. Heschel, *Israel*, 168.

Did Rabbi Heschel Influence Pope Francis?

is mutual enrichment."[32] The future pope echoed this sentiment in an interview published in 2010, when he explained that we can build a true community only recognizing the value of others and "celebrating the diversity that is enriching for us all."[33]

Pope Francis has inspired countless people of diverse religions and of no religion to seek a path and find a way toward spiritual enrichment. Perhaps through him some of the signature insights of Rabbi Abraham Joshua Heschel are reaching far more people than Heschel could have ever imagined.

32. Heschel, "No Religion," 125.
33. Bergoglio, *Pope Francis*, 234.

Bibliography

Agus, Jacob B. "Context and Challenge–A Response." In *Bulletin* 48:2 (1968): 38.
Ahmann, Mathew, ed. *Race: Challenge to Religion*. Chicago: Henry Regnery, 1963.
Ambrogetti, Francesca, and Sergio Rubin. *Pope Francis: His Life in His Own Words*. Translated by Laura Dail Literary Agency, Inc. New York: G.P. Putnam's Sons, 2013.
Baldwin, Lewis V. *To Make the Wounded Whole: The Cultural Legacy of Martin Luther King, Jr.* Minneapolis, MN: Fortress, 1992.
Bamberger, Bernard J. *The Bible: A Modern Jewish Approach*. New York: Schocken, 1963.
Bergoglio, Jorge Mario. "A Big Heart Open to God: The Exclusive Interview with Pope Francis." Interviewed by Antonio Spadaro (SJ). *America* (2013): 32.
———. *The Joy of the Gospel: Evangelii Gaudium*. Washington, DC: United States Conference of Catholic Bishops. Vatican City: Libretia Editrice Vaticana, 2013.
———. *Sobre el cielo y la tierra*. Edited by Diego F. Rosemberg. Mondadori: Random House, 2010.
Bergoglio, Jorge Mario, and Abraham Skorka. *On Heaven and Earth*. Translated by Alejandro Bermudez and Howard Goodman. New York: Random House, 2013.
Berrigan, Daniel. *To Dwell in Peace: An Autobiography*. San Francisco: HarperCollins, 1988.
Bokser, Ben Zion. "The Bible, Rabbinic Tradition and Modern Judaism," *The Bulletin* 48:2 (Spring 1968): 16.
Brown, Robert McAfee Brown, Abraham J. Heschel, and Michael Novak, eds. *Vietnam: Crisis of Conscience*. New York: Association, 1967.

Bibliography

Buber, Martin. *Eclipse of God: Studies in Relation between Religion and Philosophy.* New York: Harper Torchbooks, 1957.

———. *The Origin and Meaning of Hasidism.* Edited and translated by Maurice Friedman. New York: Harper and Row, 1960.

Calbezon, Jose Ignacio, ed. *The Bodhgaya Interviews.* Ithaca, NY: Snow Lion, 1988.

Dalai Lama, The. *See* Gyatso, Tenzin.

Davies, W. D. "Conscience, Scholar, Witness." *America* (March 10, 1973): 214.

Diamond, Eliezer. *Holy Men and Hunger Artists: Fasting and Asceticism in Rabbinic Culture.* New York: Oxford University Press, 2004.

Dresner, Samuel H. *Prayer and Politics: The Twin Poles of Abraham Joshua Heschel.* Edited by Joshua Stampfer. Portland, OR: Institute for Judaic Studies, 1985.

Efros, Israel I. *Ancient Jewish Philosophy: A Study in Metaphysics and Ethics.* Detroit: Wayne State University Press, 1964.

Embree, Ainslie T., ed. *The Hindu Tradition: Readings in Oriental Thought.* New York: Vintage, 1972.

Etkes, Immanuel. *Rabbi Israel Salanter and the Mussar Movement: Seeking the Torah of Truth.* Philadelphia: The Jewish Publication Society, 1993.

Even-Chen, Alexander. "God's Omnipotence and Presence in Abraham Joshua Heschel's Philosophy." *Shofar* Vol. 26 No. 1 (Fall 2007).

Fackenheim, Emil. *The Philosophy of Martin Buber.* Edited by Paul Arthur Schilpp and Maurice Friedman. La Salle, IL: Open Court, 1967.

———. *To Mend the World: Foundations of Post-Holocaust Thought.* Bloomington, IN: Indiana University Press, 1994.

Finkelstein, Louis, ed. *The Jews: Their History, Culture, and Religion.* New York: Harper Brothers, 1949.

Fisher, Eugene J. "Heschel's Impact on Catholic-Jewish Relations." In *No Religion Is an Island: Abraham Joshua Heschel and Interreligious Dialogue.* Edited by Harold Kasimow and Byron L. Sherwin. Maryknoll, NY: Orbis, 1991.

Flender, Harold. "Conversation with Dr. Abraham Joshua Heschel." *Women's American Ort Reporter* (January/February 1971): 3.

Fraade. Steven D. "Ascetical Aspects of Ancient Judaism." In *Jewish Spirituality: From the Bible through the Middle Ages.* Edited by Arthur Green. New York: Crossroad, 1986.

Francis (Pope). *See* Bergoglio, Jorge Mario.

Friedman, Maurice. *Abraham Joshua Heschel and Elie Wiesel: You Are My Witnesses.* New York: Farrar, Straus, and Giroux, 1987.

———. "Abraham Heschel among Contemporary Philosophers: From Divine Pathos to Prophetic Action." *Philosophy Today* (Winter 1974): 303.

———. "Abraham Joshua Heschel: Toward a Philosophy of Judaism." *Conservative Judaism* 10: 2 (Winter 1956): 2.

———. *Encyclopedia Judaica,* Vol. 4. New York: Macmillan, 1972.

———. "Liberal Judaism and Contemporary Jewish Thought." *Midstream* (Autumn 1959): 24.

Bibliography

———. *Martin Buber: The Life of Dialogue*. New York: Harper Torchbooks, 1960.

———. *To Deny Our Nothingness: Contemporary Images of Man*. New York: Delta, 1968.

———. *Touchstones of Reality: Existential Trust and the Community of Peace*. New York: E.P. Dutton, 1972.

Ginzberg, Louis. *Students, Scholars, and Saints*. New York: Meridian, 1960.

Goshen-Gottstein. "Jewish-Christian Relations: From Historical Past to Theological Future." www.jcrelations.net.

Greenburg, Irving (Rabbi). *Religions in Dialogue: From Theocracy to Democracy*. Edited by Alan Race and Ingrid Shafer. Burlington, VT: Ashgate, 2002.

Guttmann, Julius. *Philosophies of Judaism: The History of Jewish Philosophy from Biblical Times to Franz Rosenzweig*. New York: Anchor, 1966.

Gyatso, Tenzin (His Holiness the Dalai Lama). *Ethics for the New Millennium*. New York: Riverhead, 1999.

Heschel, Abraham Joshua. *Disputation and Dialogue: Readings in the Jewish-Christian Encounter*. Edited by Frank E. Talmage New York: Ktav, 1975.

———. *The Earth Is the Lord's*. New York: Farrar, Straus and Giroux, 1978.

———. "The Eternal Light." *The National Broadcasting Company*. Interviewed by Rabbi Wolfe Kelman. (March 19, 1972).

———. "From Mission to Dialogue." *Conservative Judaism* (Spring 1967): 9.

———. *God in Search of Man: A Philosophy of Judaism*. New York: Farrar, Straus, and Cudahy, 1955.

———. *Heavenly Torah as Refracted through the Generations*. Edited and translated by Gordon Tucker with Leonard Levin. New York: Continuum, 2005.

———. *The Ineffable Name of God: Man: Poems in English and Yiddish*. Translated by Morton M. Leifman. New York: Continuum, 2007.

———. *The Insecurity of Freedom: Essays on Human Existence*. New York: Farrar, Straus, and Giroux, 1966.

———. "Interview at Notre Dame." In *Moral Grandeur and Spiritual Audacity: Essays: Abraham Joshua Heschel*. Edited by Susannah Heschel. New York: Farrar, Strauss, Giroux, 1996.

———. *Israel: An Echo of Eternity*. New York: Farrar, Straus and Giroux, 1987.

———. *Kotzk: In gerangl far emesdikeit [Kotzk: The Struggle for Integrity]*. Tel-Aviv: Hamenora, 1973.

———. *Man Is Not Alone: A Philosophy of Religion*. Philadelphia: The Jewish Publication Society of America, 1951.

———. *Man Is Not Alone: A Philosophy of Religion*. New York: Farrar, Straus and Young, 1951.

———. *Man's Quest for God: Studies in Prayer and Symbolism*. New York: Charles Scribner's Sons, 1954.

———. "No Religion Is an Island." *Union Seminary Quarterly Review* 21:2 (January 1966): 126.

———. *A Passion for Truth*. New York: Farrar, Straus and Giroux, 1973.

Bibliography

———. *The Prophets*. New York: Schocken, 1972.

———. "The Religious Basis of Equality of Opportunity: The Segregation of God." In *Race: Challenge to Religion*. Edited by Mathew Ahmann. Chicago: Henry Regnery, 1963.

———. "Renewal of Religious Thought." In *Theology of Renewal*, Vol. I. Edited by L. K. Shook. New York: Herder and Herder, 1968.

———. "What We Might Do Together." *Religious Education* (March-April 1967): 135.

———. *Who is Man?* Stanford, CA: Stanford University Press, 1968.

Heschel, Susannah, ed. *Moral Grandeur and Spiritual Audacity: Essays: Abraham Joshua Heschel*. New York: Farrar, Strauss, Giroux, 1996.

Heschel, Susannah. "Theological Affinities in the Writings of Abraham Joshua Heschel and Martin Luther King, Jr." *Conservative Judaism* Vol. 50 (Winter/Spring 1998): 127.

Hick, John. "The Next Step beyond Dialogue." In *The Myth of Religious Superiority: Multifaith Explorations of Religious Pluralism*. Edited by Paul F. Knitter. Maryknoll, NY: Orbis, 2005.

Isherwood, Christopher. *Ramakrishna and His Disciples*. New York: Simon and Schuster, 1965.

Jacobs, Louis. "The Doctrine of the Zaddik in the Thought of Elimelech of Lizensk." The Rabbi Louis Feinberg Memorial Lecture in Judaic Studies, University of Cincinnati, February 9, 1978.

Jakobovits, Immanuel. "The Condition of Jewish Belief: A Symposium" compiled by the editors of *Commentary Magazine* (New York: Macmillan, 1966), 112-13.

John Paul II, (Pope). See Wojtyla, Karol.

Kaplan, Edward. "Confronting the Holocaust: God in Exile." In *Holiness in Words: Abraham Joshua Heschel's Poetics of Piety*. Albany: SUNY, 1996.

———. *Spiritual Radical: Abraham Joshua Heschel in America, 1940–1972*. New Haven: Yale University Press, 2007.

Kaplan, Mordecai. *Questions Jews Ask: Reconstructionist Answers*. New York: Reconstructionist, 1956.

Kasimow, Harold, John P. Keenan, and Linda Klepinger Keenan, eds. *Beside Still Waters: Jews, Christians, and the Way of the Buddha*. Somerville, MA: Wisdom Publications, 2003,

Kasimow, Harold. *Divine-Human Encounter: A Study of Abraham Joshua Heschel*. Washington, DC: University Press of America, 1979.

———. "A Jewish Life: Abraham Joshua Heschel, A Centenary Tribute." A special edition of *Shofar* Vol. 26 No. 1 (Fall 2007).

——— and Byron L. Sherwin, eds. *No Religion Is an Island: Abraham Joshua Heschel and Interreligious Dialogue*. Maryknoll, NY: Orbis, 1991.

Katz, Dov. *The Musar Movement*. Translated by Leonard Oschry. Tel-Aviv: Orly, 1977.

Kelman, Wolfe (Rabbi). "The Eternal Light." *The National Broadcasting Company*. (March 19, 1972).

Bibliography

King, Martin Luther, Jr. "A Challenge to the Churches and Synagogues," in Mathew Ahmann, ed., *Race: Challenge to Religion*. Chicago: Henry Regnery, 1963.

———. "Conversations with Martin Luther King." *Conservative Judaism* 22 (Spring 1968), 2.

———. *The Papers of Martin Luther King, Jr., Vol. VI*. Edited by Clayborne Carson. Berkeley: University of California Press, 2007.

———. *Why We Can't Wait*. New York: New American Library, 1964.

———. *The Words of Martin Luther King, Jr.* Edited by Coretta Scott King. New York: Newmarket, 1984.

Knitter, Paul F. *Introducing Theologies of Religions*. Maryknoll, NY: Orbis, 2002.

———., ed. *The Myth of Religious Superiority: Multifaith Explorations of Religious Pluralism*. Maryknoll, NY: Orbis, 2005.

———. *One Earth Many Religions: Multifaith Dialogue and Global Responsibility*. Maryknoll, NY: Orbis, 1995.

Kogan, Michael S. "Reply." In "Toward Total Dialogue: The Next Step in Interfaith Dialogue: A Conversation in Print," a special reprint edition of *National Dialogue Newsletter* 6:2 (Winter 1990-91): 31.

Kravitz, Leonard and Kerry M. Olitzky, trans. *Pirke Avot: A Modern Commentary on Jewish Ethics*. New York: UAHC Press, 1993.

Küng, Hans. "Christianity and World Religions: Dialogue with Islam." In *Toward a Universal Theology of Religion*. Edited by Leonard Swidler. Maryknoll, NY: Orbis, 1987.

Lamm, Norman (Rabbi). *Torah; Lishmah: Torah for Torah's Sake in the Works of Rabbi Hayim of Volozhin and His Contemporaries*. Hoboken, NJ: Ktav, 1989.

Luzzato, Moses Hayyim. *Mesillat Yesharim: The Path of the Upright*. Translated by Mordecai M. Kaplan. Philadelphia: The Jewish Publication Society of America, 1966.

Maimonides, Moses. "The Epistle to Yemen." In *Crisis and Leadership: Epistles of Maimonides*. Translated by Abraham Halkin. Philadelphia: The Jewish Publication Society of America, 1985.

Merkle, John C. ed. *Abraham Joshua Heschel: Exploring His Life and Thought*. New York: Macmillan, 1985.

———. *Approaching God: The Way of Abraham Joshua Heschel*. Collegeville, MN: Liturgical, 2009.

———. *The Genesis of Faith: The Depth Theology of Abraham Joshua Heschel*. New York: MacMillan, 1985.

Merton, Thomas. *Turning toward the World: The Journals of Thomas Merton, Vol. 4 (1960-63)*. New York: Harper Collins, 1996.

Miller John H. *Vatican II: An Interfaith Appraisal: International Theological Conference*. Notre Dame, IN: University of Notre Dame Press (March 2-16, 1966).

Morinis, Alan. *Climbing Jacob's Ladder: One Man's Rediscovery of a Jewish Spiritual Tradition*. New York: Broadway, 2002.

Bibliography

Nadler, Allan. *The Faith of the Mithnagdim: Rabbinic Responses to Hasidic Rapture.* Baltimore: Johns Hopkins University Press, 1997.

Neusner, Jacob. *American Judaism: Adventure in Modernity.* New Jersey: Prentice-Hall, 1972.

Niebuhr, Reinhold. "Masterly Analysis of Faith." *New York Herald Tribune Book Review* (April 1, 1951).

Niebuhr, Ursula M. "Notes on a Friendship: Abraham Joshua Heschel and Reinhold Niebuhr." In *Abraham Joshua Heschel: Exploring His Life and Thought.* Edited by John C. Merkle. New York: Macmillan, 1985.

Nikhilananda (Swami.) *Vivekananda: A Biography.* New York: Ramakrishna-Vivekananda Center, 1953.

———, ed. *Vivekananda: The Yogas and Other Works.* New York: Ramakrishna-Vivekananda Center, 1953.

Petuchowski, Jakob. *Ever Since Sinai: A Modern View of Torah.* New York: Scribe, 1968.

Plaut, Gunther. *The Growth of Reform Judaism.* New York: World Union for Progressive Judaism, 1965.

Polner, Murray, and Naomi Goodman, eds. *The Challenge of Shalom: The Jewish Tradition of Peace and Justice.* Philadelphia: New Society, 1994.

Rabbah, Midrash. *Genesis.* Vol. 1 Translated by H. Freedman and M. Simon. London: Soncino Press, 1951.

Race, Alan. *Christians and Religious Pluralism: Patterns in the Christian Theology of Religions.* Maryknoll, NY: Orbis, 1983.

———, and Ingrid Shafer, eds. *Religions in Dialogue: From Theocracy to Democracy.* Burlington, VT: Ashgate, 2002.

Radhakrishnan, Sarvepalli. *The Concept of Man.* Edited by P.T. Raju. London: Allen and Unwin, 1960.

Rahner, Karl. "Christianity and the Non-Christian Religions." In *Christianity and Other Religions: Selected Readings.* Edited by John Hick and Brian Hebblethwaite. Philadelphia: Fortress Press, 1981.

Raskas, Bernard. *Jewish Spirituality and Ethics.* Hoboken, NJ: Ktav, 1990.

Rothschild, Fritz A. *Between God and Man: An Interpretation of Judaism.* New York: Free, 1959.

Sacks, Jonathan. *Crisis and Covenant: Jewish Thought after the Holocaust.* Manchester: Manchester University Press, 1992.

———. *The Dignity of Difference: How to Avoid the Clash of Civilizations.* London: Continuum, 2002.

———. *To Heal A Fractured World: The Ethics of Responsibility.* New York: Schocken, 2005.

Schechter, Solomon. *Aspects of Rabbinic Theology: Major Concepts of the Talmud.* New York: Schocken, 1961.

Sherwin, Byron L. *Abraham Joshua Heschel.* Atlanta: John Knox Press, 1979.

———. "Abraham Joshua Heschel." *The Torch* (Spring 1969): 7.

———. "Conceptions, Misconceptions and Implications of the Holocaust: A Jewish Perspective." *Shofar* (Summer): 1986.

Bibliography

———. *Kabbalah: An Introduction to Jewish Mysticism.* New York: Rowman and Littlefield, 2006.

———. *Workers of Wonders: A Model for Effective Religious Leadership from Scripture to Today.* Lanham, MD: Rowman and Littlefield, 2004.

Shook, L.K., ed. *Renewal of Religious Thought.* New York: Herder and Herder, 1968.

Silverstein, Shiraga, trans. *Mesillat Yesharim.* New York: Feldheim, 1966.

Smith, Wilfred Cantwell. *The Faith of Other Men.* New York: The New American Library, 1965.

Spadaro, Antonio. "A Big Heart Open to God: The Exclusive Interview with Pope Francis." *America* (2013): 32.

Spicehandler, Ezra. "The Condition of Jewish Belief: A Symposium." Compiled by the editors of *Commentary Magazine.* New York: Macmillan, 1966.

Stern, Carl. "Interview with Dr. Heschel," in *Moral Grandeur and Spiritual Audacity: Essays: Abraham Joshua Heschel.* Edited by Susannah Heschel. New York: Farrar Straus Giroux, 1996.

Swidler, Leonard, ed. *Toward a Universal Theology of Religion.* Maryknoll, NY: Orbis, 1987.

Talmage, Frank E. *Disputation and Dialogue: Readings in the Jewish-Christian Encounter.* New York: Ktav, 1975.

Tucker, Gordon. "A. J. Heschel and the Problem of Religious Certainty," *Modern Judaism: A Journal of Jewish Ideas and Experience* 29 (2000).

Weinberg, Dudley. *Understanding Jewish Prayer.* Edited by Jakob J. Petuchowski. New York: Ktav, 1972.

Weingrod, Alex. *The Saint of Beersheba.* Albany: State University of New York Press, 1990.

Wiesel, Elie. *Legends of Our Time.* New York: Holt, Rinehart and Winston, 1968.

Wojtyla, Karol (Pope John Paul II). "To Representatives of the Shinto Religion." In *Interreligious Dialogue: The Official Teaching of the Catholic Church 1963–1995.* Edited by Francesco Gioia. Boston: Pauline, 1997.

www.ingramcontent.com/pod-product-compliance
Lightning Source LLC
Chambersburg PA
CBHW050834160426
43192CB00010B/2018